HATFUL OF TIGERS

Reflections on
Art, Culture and Politics

Sergio Ramírez

Translated by D. J. Flakoll

CURBSTONE PRESS

FIRST ENGLISH EDITION, 1995
Copyright © 1986 by Sergio Ramírez
Hatful of Tigers was first published by Editorial Nueva Nicaragua,
1986 under the title *Estás en Nicaragua*
Translation copyright © 1995 by D.J. Flakoll
ALL RIGHTS RESERVED

Printed in the U.S. on acid-free paper by BookCrafters
Jacket design: Stone Graphics

Curbstone Press is a 501(c)(3) nonprofit publishing house whose
operations are supported in part by private donations and by
grants from ADCO Foundation, J. Walton Bissell Foundation, Inc.,
Witter Bynner Foundation for Poetry, Inc., Connecticut
Commission on the Arts, Connecticut Arts Endowment Fund,
Lannan Foundation, LEF Foundation, Lila Wallace-Reader's Digest
Literary Publishers Marketing Development Program,
administered by the Council of Literary Magazines and Presses,
The Andrew W. Mellon Foundation, National Endowment for the
Arts-Literature, National Endowment for the Arts International
Projects Initiative and The Plumsock Fund.

Library of Congress Cataloging-in-Publication Data

Ramírez, Sergio. 1942—
    [Estás en Nicaragua. English]
    Hatful of Tigers / by Sergio Ramírez ; translated by D. J. Flakoll.
        p. cm.
    ISBN 0-915306-98-0 : $15.00
    1. Nicaragua—History—1979-1990. 2. Nicaragua—
Description and travel. 3. Central America—Description and
travel. 4. Cortázar, Julio. 5. Ramírez, Sergio, 1942- .   I. Title.
    F1528.R349613   1995
    972.8505'3—dc20   94-23592

CURBSTONE PRESS   321 Jackson Street   Willimantic, CT 06226

CONTENTS

AFTER

for Samuel Rovinski

NOTICE TO TRAVELERS

If everything is heart and easy-going
and faces shine with noonday light,
if, in a forest of arms, children are playing,
and life has captured every street,

You aren't in Asunción or Buenos Aires,
you haven't arrived at the wrong airport,
your journey's end is not called Santiago,
its name is not Montevideo.

The wind of freedom was your pilot
and the people's compass marked your North;
how many extended hands await you,
how many women, how many children and men

Finally building the future together,
finally transfigured into themselves,
while the long night of infamy
is lost in the neglect of forgetfulness.

You saw it from the air; this is Managua,
erect among ruins, beautiful in its wasteland,
poor, like the arms it fought with,
rich, like the blood of its children.

You see, traveler, this is your open door;
the whole country is an enormous house.
No, you didn't mistake the airport:
come right in; you're in Nicaragua.

—Julio Cortázar

ENVOI

In those days of the Seven Seas, Manlio and Rabindranah, Roberto Armijo's two sons, would lean over the railing of the little balcony of their apartment in Colonia Sacamil to look at the hills and skies of San Salvador. This was the same balcony where Teresa their mother used to hang out the wash. Teresa also took pains to arrange the overflow of books in the narrow bedrooms, the bathroom, the small living room, even the kitchen. Roberto was his own best customer in the bookstore he managed at the university; he would set aside new arrivals before other buyers could discover them: Tagore, Neruda, Darío, Musil, Dylan Thomas, Omar Khayyam, Jorge Guillén, Miguel Hernández...

Manlio (for the poet Manlio Argueta) and Rabin-dranah (obviously for Tagore) grew up and became guerrilla fighters; Manlio fell in combat in Tegucigalpa when the FUSEP attacked an FMLN safe house; his mother Teresa was with him. They kidnapped her, she disappeared, and to this day no one knows where she is.

Rabindranah (Tagore) is Comandante Claudio of the FMLN. From the balcony, he went to the hills and Manlio went to heaven.

To Teresa, wherever she may be; to Rabindranah, where he will always be; and to Manlio, where he already is, this envoi is dedicated.

BEFORE

FEBRUARY 17, 1985 (SUNDAY)
MONTPARNASSE

Here ends the recital of all these encounters. From Julio Leparc's house in the Rue Coust de Cachan, coming out of the enchanted forest of carnivorous tropical flowers with which Marta, the painter's wife, has decorated the walls, after the Argentine barbecue with Argentine friends this Sunday, we have finally arrived at the Montparnasse cemetery without the flowers we had thought so much about buying. We would have liked to describe to Julio, we would have liked to describe to Carol:

a) The mysterious trip through Paris at midnight to meet Roberto Matta in his ultrasecret study located in the ancient residence of a notable of the revolution (the French, not the Sandinista). The studio, with its dark entrance hall, its interior court and its three stories, is situated near the Louvre, but I swore to Matta that I would never reveal its precise location. The street was blocked by a pile of paving stones, so we had to go around the place six times, all part of the mystery of access to it. Next to the doorbell is a written password the visitor must know beforehand unless Matta himself is waiting on the threshold to admit him.

Germana is in charge of the preparation of a red-hot spaghetti dinner which we eat at two in the morning, after so much not-eating at meetings, interviews, and official dinners. Matta is brilliant this morning, discoursing upon the philosophy of power, amidst Chinese demons, masks from Borneo, and huge Japanese horses. As we leave, he presents me with the copy he had on the table of the memoirs of the Marquise de la Rochejaquelein, wife of one of the Catholic, monarchist landowners who rose up as rebel leaders in the counterrevolutionary war of the Vendée, which broke out in 1792, only a few years after the nineteenth of July, 1789, and which, before it was put down, extended through a number of provinces: Matagalpa, Nueva Segovia, Madriz, Jinotega.

That's right. Before you can defeat the counter-revolution, you have to know it from the inside. Matta hands me the book.

b) That was just before dawn on Sunday. Early Sunday morning we go to Armando Morales's studio in the Rue des Plantes, Montparnasse. On easels and on the walls, illuminated among paint cans, rags, brushes, palette knives, appear those adult women of our infancy who, like the fruits of a lost season, were consumed by solitude: nude, they dry their faces, standing on a beach beneath a stormy sky; a train stopped under the arch of a deserted station, an old horse-drawn coach, like those we once used to see, awaits them; secret women's faces and nude women's bodies on an afternoon in Granada beside the

Great Lake of Nicaragua; a solitary horse grazes in the scrub-grass of the coast, and there is a train leaving, a coach waiting, and a victrola that might start playing in the stormy evening; and among rulers, frames, nails, paint cans, on the other wall appears General Sandino, standing with his lieutenants, Managua 1932. They have been to the Ideal Haberdashery in the Calle del Triunfo to try on shirts that the owner wants to give them in appreciation, and, as they leave, a street photographer lines them up against the pink wall of the Salon Rosado ice cream shop to take their pictures; and Armando Morales is watching them across the street from the doorway of his father's hardware store. "That is Sandino," his father points him out, and the boy paints Sandino; the street photographer takes a picture of Sandino.

c) Afterwards to Julio Leparc's workshop, which we finally locate among dingy buildings, the backs of factories, and the double doors of warehouses in the Rue de Rabats, in the suburb of Antony on the outskirts of Paris. "Are you sure this is the place?" the frightened French security official asks Ambassador Serrano. After the mysterious visit of the previous midnight, the police have had enough.

We accompany Julio Leparc through his workshop. Among the marvels of kinetic perfection in that enormous workshop that really is orderly and solid like a factory in its action and work because there is no doubt that perfection requires such apparatus, there can be heard the affable, seductive sound of a concertina playing a tango. Of course! A tango.

d) And now, finally, the cemetery on a winter afternoon.

Luis Tomasello, Julio's sculptor friend, has come with us from Leparc's house to show us the place, and he guides us through the strange agglomeration of miniature mausoleums. He cut and polished the slab. The drawing of the *cronopio* engraved on it is by Julio Silva, of course, whom you will remember from *Around the Day in Eighty Worlds*.

A few moments of silence; I stand there with my wife before the tombstone; we are numb under our overcoats in this cold February. I hear Tomasello's voice reminding Serrano that the first anniversary of Julio's death was only a few days ago, and behind us Roberto Armijo is arguing with Armando Morales as to whether César Vallejo's tomb is really here or in Père Lachaise. A mother is out for a stroll with her baby, pushing the carriage along the path that winds among the toy monuments of the cemetery.

With my hands in my coat pockets, I detect the odor of a waxed floor, high heels clicking on the wooden boards, and the foamy wake of the boat taking us to Mancarrón Island in Solentiname dissolves far away in the brilliant sunshine; the military plane lands among desolate hills on the Siuna airstrip, and you are blinded by the sparkle of ground glass on the Velero beach facing Puerto Sandino, and the peasants of Ostional who can't hear my voice, and the mothers of Belén in the shadows.

Tombs are for remembering. And one stands there in silence in order to do that, and you're going to stock your memory with all these encounters, using this simple method which consists of standing in front of a tomb and remembering.

1965. SAN JOSÉ, COSTA RICA

Why, just now, a waxed floor, the secretaries' heels clicking on the shiny boards that give off the sweetish smell of wax, and the constant patter of raindrops? The country house on the hill of San Pedro de Montes de Oca, with its countless passageways, staircases, nooks; the offices, each with its window looking out on the rain, the easy chairs upholstered in gray vinyl, my desk at the end of a dark hallway, and on my desk, among folders and regional documents of the Central American Superior University Council (CSUCA), the Argentine edition of *Bestiary,* brought to me from Buenos Aires by that Salvadoran friend who in those days aspired to be a *cronopio* but later turned into the worst kind of company man and wound up as Minister of Justice under General Molina.

Recently arrived in San José from the University of León, I was just emerging from my first methodical reading of Borges, convinced, as I closed each of those paperback volumes edited by Emece, that there was no experimental path to perfection other than perfection itself, that writing was nothing more than the linking of impeccable periodic sentences one after the other, by the magician with his hat full of snow-white rabbits.

But there was also *Bestiary*, already old (1951) and the brand new name of Cortázar, with his hat full of tigers. Did one then begin with novelty? Was perfection a novelty? To take reality apart, make it sparkle: something new was starting as a great adventure beyond the still vastness of Borges.

And, as if chance had *prepared* it for me, as chance always does prepare things, one day, walking along the central avenue of San José, umbrella in hand as I was learning to walk in that damp city, *Hopscotch* with its black cover and the weightiness of a serious book, in the window of Lehmann's bookstore. When one is twenty years old, everything weighty is serious unless someone can prove otherwise.

Hopscotch the way one would like to read it, literature being turned upside down—and just try to imagine its seductive power. May 1965 I wrote inside the front cover of that copy, now worn with handling by so many friends over the years—one was Carlos Fonseca. Twenty years later Julio pulled it from the Cortázar shelf of my library in Managua, because twenty years is nothing, and he was preparing something or reading something for one of his many formal appearances in Sandinista patios, gardens, and auditoriums, and he left his signature on the page under that date (May 1965), like the paw print of the tiger stalking from room to room.

That was how we realized that one can also create serious literature when fooling around. Language and its mechanisms, passion and its rigor, the lyric and its mystery, and the outrageous to make sure you'll never be admitted to the Academy in any of its Central American chapters: that badinage by which we educated ourselves, along with Manlio Argueta, Roberto Armijo, José Roberto Cea, and Roque Dalton—who wasn't there but who was Grand Master of the Lodge, in those noondays at the Seven Seas in San Salvador: beer oyster hopscotch lucy in the sky with diamonds, thelonius monk, Oliveira— would he ever find her? La Maga entered our lives and we all used to adore her. Rocamadour and the sentimental scene of his death, in the middle of the boisterous crowd of regulars, white-collar workers in neckties, we used to talk learnedly about secret mechanisms and "ludic" mechanisms, that little word we learned then, Cortazarian and Rayuelian, without demeaning Don Chico Gavidia. On this side, only *cronopios;* in the middle, the wannabes, and beyond them, the company men; the world was hopelessly divided by class.

There was, therefore, a Latin American literature beyond Canaima and Huasipungo, beyond the banana trilogy of Asturias (our first Central American Nobel Prize winner), beyond our venerable Saint Salarrué and his Izalco Indians. Wise conclusions—and we had also learned to distinguish between the vernacular and Juan Rulfo.

Hopscotch was a sort of antidote or universal cure-all for snakebite. If one was climbing the ladder of the Central American bureaucracy then, well-supplied with acronyms to choose from, with sure step and at such an early age, one could easily end up bitten by the snake and become a company man in a coat and tie, and once you're an executive functionary and expert international adviser, caught up in the hierarchy and its vertigo, there are no antidotes. And since then, the Cortázar years; *Los Premios* with its fresh odor and more occult mechanisms to discover. Because it was not only the joy of reading and being free to read, or knowing oneself free to write, but it was all those meshed gears that one had to take apart at each reading, to learn the function of the connecting rods and the uses of the cranks, the properties of the springs in the clockwork mechanism, *62 modelo para armar,* and so many other prizes.

(By that time, the *boom* was beginning to make its way into the bookshop run by Roberto Armijo in the university city of San Salvador, first drop by drop and then in torrents like water from a broken main).

DAGUERREOTYPE

The copy of *Hopscotch* passed through Carlos Fonseca's hands, as already mentioned. Between July and October of 1965, ascending San Pedro hill on identical rainy afternoons, with indistinct figures carrying black umbrellas, Carlos Fonseca would walk into the offices of CSUCA almost every day, also with umbrella in hand as if it were part of his clandestine getup. During the long evening sessions we talked about the rural reality of Nicaragua, of the FSLN's work in organizing the peasants, and also about Sandino; and naturally we talked about Rubén Darío—when didn't we? Carlos spent long hours in the National Library investigating the poet's Costa Rican sojourn at the behest of Don Edelberto Torres, who, from his Mexican exile, continued to write his *Dramatic Life of Rubén Darío.* Don Julian Marchena, the elderly director of the library, was a *most* Costa Rican poet who eagerly provided Carlos with everything for his Darían labors, bringing books and papers to the desk in the corner of the reading room where Carlos was also writing his documents about armed struggle and the revolution; don't say that wasn't a real dialectical complementarity!

But in the CSUCA afternoons we talked as well about committed and uncommitted writers, useful and useless literary games, and the new Latin American novel that was beginning to make waves. And Carlos—stammering and meditative, his heavy body thrust forward in the gray vinyl armchair, elbows on knees, nylon windbreaker damp with rain, his stern eyes half closed for long intervals when he left off talking about the revolution in order to keep on thinking about it—also cured me of the poison: the risk of turning into a company man.

A CONVERSATION ABOUT
CENTRAL AMERICA
IN THE "SEVEN SEAS"

To discover Central America, to learn to understand her and to love her, seriously to grasp that concept which is so often banal, abstract, and foolish: Central America, to which we will later return and which is not a Rotarian or Lions' Club membership in the one big homeland, becomes concrete each September fifteenth—so concrete that it has a cutting edge that can hurt you and if you don't think so, remember the Minerva cults of the venerable Don Manuel Estrada Cabrera: pubescent flower girls offering him acanthus leaves; poetry competitions directed by the distinguished bard José Santos Chocano, and Greek temples glimpsed by Huxley from a train window in the middle of the tropical jungle; Guatemala under the Athenian boot of Estrada Cabrero—and even today the Indians from the hills around Chichi-castenango, if they are carrying nothing in their *cacaxtles* when they return home to their hamlets from a day at the marketplace posing for tourist cameras, will pick up rocks beside the road to fill the pack frames in order to feel the weight and tautness of the *mecapal* straps across

25

their foreheads while they climb the steep highway snaking among the forested hills.

Estrada Cabrera was the one who invented clandestine cemeteries; later others invented the death squads, and still others the strategic villages; of my friends at the University of San Carlos in the sixties, not one is left: all disappeared, kidnapped, buried in clandestine cemeteries, machine-gunned as they got into their cars or approached the school entrance to pick up their children; I've seen their last photos so many times in *El Gráfico,* crumpled over the steering wheel, the windshield shattered, the head bloodied. Firemen coming down the hillside bearing a stretcher, coming out of the brush carrying the body of the artist with whom in Mixco you watched a new day dawn. It was another who took you to his small ranch in Purulha where the *quetzal* used to appear, magical and tiny amid the foliage, but only once in a while; and now he too is dead.

The Central America of the colonels trained at Fort Gulick was springing then not only from literature but from life itself, and from the death that inspired the literature. And Chema López Valdizón? The humble storywriter always wearing a necktie that made him look like an unlucky insurance salesman, who used to visit me in the old Panamerican Hotel on Sixth Avenue in Guatemala City and take me riding in the incredible car he had built himself from parts he found in junkyards and automobile graveyards: Chema, who disappeared one day, his strange vehicle left on the highway, looking even stranger without driver or passengers: kidnapped, disappeared, dead, writer, subversive. And what about Otto René Castillo and Roque Dalton?

It was definitely worthwhile being a writer in Central America, and that was the essence of the ludic: that the game was for keeps and is for keeps, far from abstract; the passion for the living and the rancor of the real.

OCTOBER 1967, LEÓN, NICARAGUA

In the university auditorium, among portraits of priests, founding fathers, and academics, the place where the student demonstration started on July 23, 1959, the afternoon when we were massacred by gunfire from Somoza's National Guard, we inaugurate a seminar on *Hopscotch* and the literary "boom."

It is a serious seminar, opened by the rector. One cannot speak except with academic solemnity in this hall where we also began the hunger strike and the sit-in of September 1959 after the massacre; we took over the university and nailed its doors shut from inside to demand the expulsion of National Guard officials registered as students.

Nocturnal bombs, searches, prisoners, slogans painted on the walls, bonfires. The University lights are always burning, the mimeograph machines working; 1967 is the year of Pancasán, the greatest test yet of the FSLN in the mountains. We are explaining the new trend and speaking of the new narrative during the days and nights of Pancasán, the time when the Sandinista spark was being fanned into distant bonfires.

Thirty students from León and Managua have registered to participate in the seminar, and we have done everything in an orderly and timely fashion; it is to be a discussion based on prior knowledge, and the participants have already received their copies of *Hopscotch, The Death of Artemio Cruz, Pedro Páramo* and *The City and the Dogs.* Pancasán, the clandestine cells; more than a few of the participants are conspirators, and some enter the hall furtively.

After the sessions, we resume the conversation about novels, commitment, the writer, literature, revolution, with Jaime Wheelock, a law student who is participating in the seminar; midnight finds us in the Ventana bar; it is the time when the Guards make their rounds, the time for house searches and arrests. The Ventana is located on Calle Real on the way to Subtiava, and this year—the year of Fernando Gordillo's death—we could boast that this *cantina* with its four tottering tables in a patio of *chagüite* and lemon trees has been named in honor of the Ventana poets, the *Ventana Review,* the youthful literary movement that Gordillo and I began in 1960.

Nineteen sixty-seven, the year of Pancasán, of the hundredth anniversary of Rubén Darío, of the massacre in the streets of Managua of peasants enticed there that January 22nd for the electoral trap of conservative boss Fernando Agüero, who, before making a deal with Somoza, aspired to beat him in fair elections, no less; the year of Fernando Gordillo's death.

Che Guevara fell in Bolivia; the radios repeat the news in the street, in the hot night that enters with its warm breath through the balconies of the auditorium's half-open windows.

And Pancasán, the glow of bonfires, the distant rumble, the first faint ray of dawn beneath the closed door.

DAGUERREOTYPE

On April 3, 1970, Luisa Amanda Espinoza was assassinated in León, along with Enrique Lorenzo Ruiz; both clandestine militants of the FSLN. "Nest of Communists Uncovered!" read the headline in the daily *Novedades* the following day; and in the photo, carefully arranged by Somoza's security agents, were the objects found in the house on the Ermita de Dolores that served them as a refuge: a few pistols, an old carbine perhaps, magazines, military training pamphlets, manifestos, fliers, a flashlight, and a copy of *Hopscotch.* Subversive literature, according to *Novedades.*

Today, April 3, 1985, I have seen Luisa Amanda's photo reproduced in *El Nuevo Diario* as another anniversary of her death rolls around; her schoolgirl face, innocent and simple, she looks as if she has just stepped out of the shower. The security police followed the two of them through the streets, and they didn't lose their cool even though they knew the killers were at their heels.

Rogelio tells me that he had left the house where Camilo Ortega was hiding to look for another safe house, because the Guard might arrive at any moment. Those were the days when there were few safe houses and few collaborators. It surprised him to find Luisa Amanda in the street, looking anxiously for a taxi; she only paused to ask him to note the license number of the cab as she got into it. Everything was happening at once. Five minutes later, when Rogelio entered his office in the Guardian Agricultural Service to try to make a contact by telephone, the secretary told him there had just been a shooting, a girl was dead, and it hadn't even been five minutes. Was it possible or had it been a dream? Not even five minutes since he had met her in the street, since she had taken the cab, and the secretary in his office already had the news that Luisa Amanda was dead; she had gotten out of the cab, found Enrique walking down the street; the agents had followed her, caught up with her and shot her, all in the time it had taken Rogelio—who was hurrying—to walk to his office, and there had still been time enough for the rumor that Luisa Amanda was dead to reach the secretary.

Those were not easy days, but days of composure, self-possession, calm, as you walked down the street pretending to be cool, while the jeep crept along behind you and the agents on foot crossed the intersections discreetly, keeping their distance. Luisa Amanda wasn't even twenty years old: a woman, a girl, a child. Our girl, the apple of our eye, the kid, the woman, the AMNLAE. She entered—they both entered—a patio, an unfamiliar house. The jeeps sped up then, the agents started running, shots rang out, a burst of automatic fire, another, and in the offices of the Guardian Agricultural Service they already knew that both had been killed.

She walks serenely, tranquil, under the burning sun, and they follow her through the city streets, *Hopscotch* among her subversive belongings.

What was the "boom" doing, getting mixed up in those things?

SUMMER 1974. EAST BERLIN

A missed encounter with Julio Cortázar, but an
encounter with Antonio Skármeta. Propelled by the
winds of exile, Antonio had arrived in West Berlin months
before, along with many other Chileans, including
journalists, professors, folklorists, singers, university
students: all the scattered and active diaspora following
the coup of September 1973; but Antonio was the
exceptional exile, always flat broke. The other exile who
was just as exceptional was Ariel Dorfmann who didn't
get stranded in Berlin and only came rushing through
like the Flying Dutchman he had become.

Antonio with his delight in life; despite all his
disasters and torments, he breathed in the joy of living
sensually, through his nostrils. From bedazzlement I
progressed to frank admiration for his irrepressible
worship of the ladies, all kinds of ladies. I couldn't help
praising and admiring him, my life in Berlin being as it
was, more tranquil, domestic, and calm, seated eight
hours a day before my typewriter in the studio on
Helmstedterstrasse in Wilmersdorf, an old neighborhood
of middle-class Jews. As a scholarship holder I was forced
to type away as if I were a stenographer.

From our first encounter, we were friends, most of all, I think, because of Antonio's love and respect for the bolero *Sinceridad,* which Lucho Gatica sang in his better days and which until then Antonio, like so many other Latin Americans, hadn't known was the inspired creation of the Nicaraguan Gastón Pérez, alias "Donkey's Ear."

It was Antonio who arranged a date for me to meet Julio Cortázar on the other side, in East Berlin, when he had to come to the Democratic Republic of Germany because of some seminar or congress. It must have been about June 1974, and the meeting was arranged for a Sunday afternoon.

I had to prepare myself mentally for that encounter; after all, I was the typical disciple going in search of his master. What I mean is that I thought a lot about how to conduct the interview: what intellectual baggage I should display, my ideas about literature; in brief, I wanted to make a good impression in artistic terms: this kid is promising and maybe afterwards a prologue. With my books under my arm, as was fitting, I got off at the Friederichstrasse station and, filled with the illusions, uneasiness, hopes, and fears of one who ventures into the great unknown, I walked down Unter den Linden toward Alexanderplatz, where his hotel was located.

(This first meeting couldn't result in anything but an intimate and cordial friendship for the simple reason that, since Antonio and I were such good friends and had so much in common, Cortázar couldn't continue to be such a good friend of Antonio's without becoming an intimate friend of mine; the triangle couldn't be left open at that corner.

Cortázar waiting for me, seated on a sofa in the hotel lobby, frowning slightly and as ageless as he appeared on the dust jackets, tall and with extremely long legs because he kept growing every day, and, since he loved his cat, Teodoro Adorno, so much, he almost certainly would have brought him along to Berlin and would be stroking the cat's head while he awaited me).

At the reception desk they told me he was out, he hadn't returned. The room tag of his key was visible in his pigeonhole, immobile, unfeeling.

There actually was a sofa, and I sat down to wait for him. A Chilean exile sat next to me, also with his books under his arm; he was doing the same thing I was, and the fact that there were two of us didn't make us feel any better; was this going to be a public meeting, an intimate conversation, or what? The sofa was strategically placed so we would see him as soon as he entered; we exchanged a few words but without showing each other the books we carried; instead, we pretended we weren't carrying any books. One of us would get up from time to time without saying anything to the other and make a furtive sortie into the reception desk's territory. The key remained there imperturbably; nobody could have removed it without our knowledge.

The hours passed, and nothing. Did it start to get dark? Finally, the Chilean and I, encouraged by the solidarity that develops from joint frustration that removes all competitive spirit, decided to leave the books in his pigeonhole and, after commenting reproachfully on his informality, we left the hotel, each going his separate way; I returned to the train station; the theory of the triangle fell apart, and Cortázar remained a phantom, along with his cat.

A CHAT ABOUT
CENTRAL AMERICAN UNION
IN THE "SEVEN SEAS"

Central America as a scholarly myth, Central America as a dream of third-class public offices. What existed were the brittle fragments of that shattered crystal, splinters that wounded; and already the powerful owners of the fragments were there (coffee-growing generals, cattle-ranching ministers, businessmen presidents), who along the dusty roads had ordered the construction of barrack-room palaces from which to govern.

The powerful were no longer interested in Central American union, Morazán's swollen horse rotted away in a curve of one of those distant bridle paths, and when the Colossus of the North appeared on the scene, they were even less interested. From then on, Central America seems more like a bicycle wheel than a bicycle chain. The good neighbor is in the center of the wheel, naturally, and our little countries, tiny and sweet supplicants, are the spokes converging toward this center. The national bourgeoisie (the term is all right for lack of a better one, but Roque always thought it was too grand a compliment to designate as bourgeoisie the bosses who fart in drawing

38

rooms). They don't want to be the strongly united links of a chain. No, either spokes joined to the hub of the wheel, or nothing at all.

Morazán on horseback, galloping all over Central America to uncover the vestry uprisings of the powerful. He knew (and that's why the rich nicknamed him "Chico Ganzúa" to imply that he was only a vulgar thief and not a general on horseback) that Central America made no sense unless it was united; but the rich also knew that from the beginning; they wanted the Spanish crown or nothing, and after that they wanted the Yankee or nothing. They yearned for the Yankee even before the Yankee showed up, and they weren't happy until they shot Morazán off his horse. That task fell to the *ticos*, who have the reputation of never firing a shot, but since they are also the tropical heirs of the Swiss canton culture, they later named a park after him: Morazán Park in San José.

The Yankees' best ally and sworn enemy of Morazán was General Carrera of Guatemala. It's true that the Yankees didn't yet exist in these parts, but, great visionary that he was, he knew they'd be coming, and he was their greatest ally. When one comes to realize that the Carreras can really win out against the Morazáns, there's no choice but to live with your rifle cocked and at the ready.

And how many Carreras have been engendered since then: toads suckling on vestry milk, venomous company men. It was only Carrera whom the wealthy called an "illiterate Indian" without meaning to be offensive, but rather as a sort of tribute: Carrera didn't rise up against the bosses to cut their throats; rather, he was trained in the sacristies to cut throats in the name of the bosses, and his example later inspired Estrada Cabrera and after that General Ubico, and everything that has been done since then in Guatemala in the name of God, the fatherland, the family, and religion comes from way back there.

With the idea of Central American union discarded, as a consequence of the geopolitical concept of the bicycle wheel, the rich and powerful continued to permit references to "the great homeland," but only on the fifteenth of September, Independence Day. Central America came to be a sentimental feeling, a scholarly nostalgia transmitted by grade-school teachers with chalk dust on their ties, a teachers' college dream: the great homeland, one flag, one anthem, *La Granadera*.

Philosophical theories about Central American union are hotly debated at Rotarian and Lions' Club meetings, sessions of the Salvadoran Athenaeum, and symposia of the Padre Trino Academy in Tegucigalpa, as well as at Masonic lodge meetings and rallies of the Central American Unionist Party; heated discussions take place regarding the most desirable location for the federal capital of Central America, and two positions prevail: a new capital city in the Gulf of Fonseca, on the Island of Tigre, Meanguera, or Meanguerita. The borders of at least three Central American countries converge on the gulf, namely Nicaragua, Honduras, and El Salvador, and as a powerful additional argument, the Gulf of Fonseca is destined to become a future center of world commerce and mercantile activity.

(What a nuisance, the theory of the bicycle wheel. The possibility of establishing the capital of Central America on the Gulf of Fonseca is seriously interrupted, as these words are being written, by the formidable presence of the Colossus of the North in this Central American region, mainly in the territories that belong to our sister republic of Honduras: a swarm of radar beacons beneath the thick clouds over the gulf and flights of planes that stain the celestial blue).

The alternative is to designate one of the present capitals of the nations involved as the federal capital, but this possibility, unfortunately, is undermined by the following objections:

Guatemala: The largest, most modern city. Its urbanization plan was inspired by Hausmann, who also designed eternal Paris. The inconvenience: the Guatemalans still think they are the captain generals of the kingdom.

San Salvador: The progress that its children have brought to it makes it an extremely modern and cosmopolitan city. Outstanding among its public monuments is a statue of the Savior of the World standing upon the terrestrial globe. The problem: this country is incredibly small.

Tegucigalpa: A picturesque city, though undeveloped. Outstanding among its modern constructions is the

Tiburcio Carías Andino Stadium as well as the sanctuary of the Virgin of Suyapa. The problem: the Hondurans are very slow-witted.

Managua: An ugly, slovenly city; destroyed by an earthquake in 1931, it has the disadvantage of being subject at any moment to more earthquakes; and one must also keep in mind the turbulent and insubordinate character of the Nicaraguans.

San José: Favored by the opportune European immigration that brought a refreshing breath of civilization and orderly labor to this small country; we can certainly say that San José is like a little silver cup, with its monumental National Theater, of which Costa Rica is justly proud, and why not all Central America as well? It is fitting that Costa Rica should enjoy, in addition to its gentle and beneficent climate, the nickname "the Central American Switzerland." The problem: the Costa Ricans themselves.

A united Central America.

How much time must he have spent seated at his desk, table, or lectern, how many hours of sleeplessness and pain in the spinal column? But Don Salvador Mendieta completed the seven volumes of his *The Sickness of Central America,* a didactic monument to Central American union.

And we also have the form and philosophy of Don Alberto Masferrer, the inspired thought of Professor Juan José Arévalo, the only schoolteacher who ever occupied the presidential chair, and who also had clear-cut unionist ideas, although because of his rejection of communism he has seen fit to support the Guatemalan military now, in the twilight of his life.

Central American union. Painstakingly to comb the snake, the happy and contented snake wearing a hair ribbon. And the bicycle wheel turns. To be sure we have removed a spoke from the wheel, but it still turns.

APRIL 1976.
SAN JOSÉ / SOLENTINAME

Julio Cortázar's Costa Rican trip and his first entrance into Nicaragua by way of the San Juan River. We are finally going to meet on this side. I have finished my Berlin stay and have returned with my draft of *Did the Blood Scare You?* at the call of the FSLN. He wasn't in Paris either, when I passed through, loaded down with suitcases, in the summer of 1975, and we talked about Cortázar again, with Ariel Dorfmann and Roberto Armijo, in an Algerian restaurant in the Latin Quarter: the pursuit of the phantom continued.

Everything was ready for his series of lectures on literature in the National Theater—the little table, the chair, and the glass of water on the same stage where in other times the great Costa Rican tenor Melico Salazar, rival of Enrico Caruso, used to sing. Behind him, the flies, the stage machinery, and at his feet the orchestra seats; at the rear the semicircle of boxes with their golden reliefs; in the dome above, the Neoclassic Italian frescoes, all of it a legitimate source of national pride.

Samuel Rovinski had spent several days trying to sensitize Costa Rican intellectual opinion to the Cortázar phenomenon by means of a series of introductory lectures. I don't think his efforts were very successful because there was the theater full of umbrellas, but why do you write, for pleasure or for commitment, and what do you think of the repression of writers in the Soviet Union, the *gulag,* and the horrors of cultural Stalinism, and are you a communist or not?

Umbrellas, broken sidewalks, pots of palm hearts cooking on the street corners, intellectuals with umbrellas, and you might have been one of them, Spanish grammarians and Greco-Roman poets, the Athens of Central America; all the city buses proudly bore on their sides the rampant eagle of the USA coat of arms, *e pluribus unum,* and explain that to me, man.

Julio was taking a shower in his room at the Hotel Europa while I was waiting for him that dawn to leave for the San Juan River, to whisk him away from the deadly dullness of San José, in complicity with Oscar Castillo, flying in a light plane in the sunny morning toward the very border of Nicaragua, landing bumpily among the grass and stones of the airstrip at Los Chiles, now a modern military airport three thousand meters long—one meter for each inhabitant of Los Chiles—which General Paul Gormann, chief of the southern command, personally inspected when the US Army Corps of Engineers had completed the construction work—so times change.

Las Brisas, the border estate of the Coronel family beside the Medio Queso River, a tributary of the San Juan.

The flatlands are swampy, peaceful, without a breath of air, and from the hill of the ranch house one can see in the distance the Medio Queso snaking its way from the Costa Rican lowlands to empty into the San Juan.

We are going to go down the Medio Queso in the motorboat, navigating among the green clumps of grass that the current pushes toward the propeller, coming out into the wide reaches of the San Juan, leaving behind the frontier post of Fátima, to disembark at Santa Fe on the other bank, and once more in the motorboat to bypass San Carlos, and from there to the open waters of the lake toward the peaceful islands of the archipelago whose gentle promontories can be seen in the distance.

Julio Cortázar entered Nicaragua then for the first time in April 1976 by the clandestine gateway of Los Chiles/Las Brisas/the Medio Queso River/Santa Fe/the San Juan River/the Great Lake of Nicaragua/Solentiname. There are instant Polaroid pictures as souvenirs of that trip, which must still be in the possession of Doña María at the Las Brisas ranch house; there are Julio's own photos of primitive paintings, children, landscapes; and a picture taken by Oscar Castillo in the doorway of the Solentiname church in which Ernesto Cardenal, Julio, and I appear—with me still wearing my writer's mustache from the Berlin days.

Somewhere, perhaps next to the side door of the little church, I hold up the primitive paintings so Julio can photograph them in the first light of the morning, and I think: even great writers have a touch of the gringo tourist. Is he taking pictures of these paintings out of a sense of folklore, the primitivism so dear to European cultural concepts, as a hunting trophy of a journey through the tropics? But don't forget the apocalypse, and stop fooling around with folklore, little calves, little houses, and stars in a too-blue sky, because that was probably the only paint they had. The important thing is the apocalypse.

(And that solid, unblemished friendship from then on, talking to you as though you had never stopped seeing each other and as if it weren't your first encounter, the sort of rewarding friendship that you'd been seeking ever since childhood when the new boy who is spending his school vacation in town dazzles you in the park with his tricks on the bicycle and your yearning to become his friend, hovering around him, following him at a distance when he goes back to the mysterious house where he is staying with his parents, and suddenly there we are talking, you take him home and he even lends you his bicycle, and you go to the movies together.)

Back in San José before his departure, he leaves me a declaration of solidarity with the struggle of the FSLN, his first written statement of support, which along with his signature is somewhere among my papers from those days, coded messages, drafts of manifestos, clandestine proclamations, cross correspondence: the pinched, left-handed scrawl of Humberto (Pedro Antonio), the typewritten missives in thick red letters from Jaime (Julio), the hard years when the Front was divided, my own pseudonym in the messages (Baltazar), chosen out of love for Durrell; and the declaration, cleanly typed by Julio on his portable typewriter in the hotel room.

1976. Later that same year Carlos Fonseca would fall, Eduardo Contreras would fall.

DAGUERREOTYPE

Las Brisas. We might have run into Eduardo Contreras around there; during those months he was clandestine around the big lake, navigating for hours in barges that carried cattle from Santa Fe to Diamante in Granada: old landing craft from the second world war bought as scrap in New Orleans and used as floating corrals.

He had directed the assault on Chema Castillo's house in Managua on December 27, 1974, and before leaving for the airport with his hostages, the elegant ladies who had swallowed their jewels in terror when the guerrillas burst in, finally had the opportunity of seeing his face when he took off his stocking mask, the face of a screen idol which no one had seen before and no one remembered. Cultivated, they would repeat in amazement afterwards, polite, educated, persuasive, suggestive. How could it be that he should speak English, that he should speak German, that he should know philosophy, that he should know literature, and be at the same time so firm, so quick, so implacable, so self-assured in his command of the situation, placing each man at his post, relieving the sentries, ordering them to fire, ordering

49

them not to surrender when he was negotiating by telephone with Somoza himself while all the guards were surrounding the house? He had bewildered them, seduced them, none of them could deny it; a shiver, astonishment, the sensual need to obey. The other masked men called him Marcos, Comandante Zero, and who was not going to obey him?

And he was still sensual, tough, firm, fiery, and resolute when he was lying in the drawer of the morgue; he had not stopped giving orders even when he was stretched out in the drawer of the morgue, when he was lying on the deck of the barge navigating secretly under the stars in the immensity of the dark lake, the huge black expanse of water and the tireless motor pushing the barge along amid the lowing of the cattle, the barge passing the islands of the archipelago of Solentiname under the burning midday sun, and far to the south the distant mountains of Costa Rica, leaving the river behind, the peaceful flatlands without a breath of air, the flooded grassland, the green clumps of *gamalotes* swaying in the current.

Eduardo Contreras passed by here, here he slept and ate, he was here; this river saw him, this lake, these islands, this shore.

IN WHICH THERE IS MORE TALK ABOUT CENTRAL AMERICA IN THE "SEVEN SEAS"

With the passage of time, Central America became a pretty fruitless idea in political terms; all epic feeling of distant wars for federation that General Francisco Morazán waged after independence from Spain and in which some liberal chieftains engaged even until the end of the 19th century was lost; the provinces which were still dominated by uncouth oligarchies could not yield on a greater geographical and historical level; we might have had our manifest destiny which was to be united, but it was already clear that only that other destiny was manifest, that of the Colossus.

Central America lost its respectability, and from then on, filibusters, pirates, buccaneers, bankers, banana company managers, Yankee ambassadors, or American ministers as they were called in those days, hired and fired presidents, bought and sold representatives, imposed and suppressed laws; the bicycle wheel was beginning to spin. Our scattered and discordant handful of countries, so often pushed to fight amongst ourselves by the fruit companies or the bankers, occupied by the military and governed by folklore insanity, were delivered, exhausted and alone, to the fate of having to sell their traditional agricultural products and themselves to the highest bidder, the only bidder. There was only one buyer.

The political dispersal, the uselessness of economic enforcement and the impossibility of accomplishing national projects in such tiny segments, provoked, as a consequence, the stratification of a provincial life-style which in turn formed a kind of cultural behavior: the cultural behavior of servility, impotence and conformity with the mediocre, the exaltation of rhyme, padding, repetition, a kind of self-satisfied drowsiness and smudged cliché that perceived backwardness as novelty, anachronism of forms and syncretism of the secondhand and the rejected, a delirious love of pomposity and the masturbatory vice of rhetoric, the consecration of oratory as an art in itself, as if the words served only to repeat high-flown phrases, the dissonance of folklore and the spinelessness of the vernacular corrupting the popular warp and woof of the culture, provincial Central America closed in on itself, raising around itself the high walls of vulgarity, our own brand of kitsch which was growing every day, feeding on excrescences. The rich had no nation; nor were they interested in one.

Not even the forced modernization itself introduced by the Alliance for Progress at the onset of the decade of the sixties, common market and free interchange of merchandise, was ever capable of creating any sort of new impulse, although the rich were taught to recognize each other across the sad Central American borders. Huge feudal estates beneath the smoke of the chimneys—all that great imposture took none of the piggishness away from the rich and powerful no matter how often the Salvadoran barons brought Pablo Casals to give concerts in San Salvador and Doña Hope Somoza raised her monumental national theater in the *miasma* of the Lake of Managua. There was no possible artifice by which the rich and powerful could rescue Central America from the mediocrity they themselves had stamped upon it, especially if we remember that they were already living in Miami in spirit, and that the cultural revival was now forcing the imposition of an even more degraded subculture, the worm in the apple.

(It occurs to me that the coffee barons brought Casals to San Salvador as they might have brought José Feliciano to the Santa Tecla country fair, because when Doña Hope brought Victoria de los Angeles to Managua she asked her to put *Granada* by Agustín Lara on the program amid her operatic repertoire; and her theater was inaugurated with a concert by Tony Aguilar, rooster in hand and silver spurs on his heels, and, if you don't believe me, there is *Novedades* to keep me from lying about it.)

There is no doubt that with the Alliance for Progress the rich and powerful felt better connected to the center of the bicycle wheel, but even so, their sense of political relationship remained provincial, and certainly brutal. General Miguel Ydígoras Fuentes did push-ups in his regular calisthenic appearances before the TV cameras of Guatemala, just as General Hernández Martínez, thirty years earlier, had broadcast daily over the radio his teaching about magnetic fluids, but that is folklore; reality came to be the death squads and the anti-communist lodges: the White Hand is the cultural product of the rich, par excellence.

Disappearances, kidnappings, clandestine prisons, secret graveyards: a Central American product made in Guatemala, sold in El Salvador. Other products such as Somoza and his whole Miami court were assembled right in the United States.

Isolation, deformity, distortion. The backwardness established by dependence becomes tenacious and dominates everything, from the rhetorical cynicism in political behavior to the provincial coloration of republican operettas, to the repression sanctified in courtrooms where hens lay eggs on the piles of old record books, police stations that look like mosques, khaki-colored government palaces, poetry competitions, Darían soirées, musty athenaeums, Central American shabbiness in Salvadoran cultural supplements which carry the sonnets of David Escobar Galindo next to the crossword puzzle. In Honduras we still haven't gotten around to abstract art. How could we, if we were still unacquainted with the concrete?

Central American categories, reflections in dammed-up water, impossibility, impotence. Central American culture is a stagnant passion, and around it rise high, circular walls, barring access to the universal; the Central

American seen as universal through the telescope of underdevelopment, which is so integral that it has no cracks; from wherever you may see it, it is beckoning to you. And the owners of the telescope proudly lend it to whoever wants to peer through the fogged lens to look at dead things.

Central American culture.

SEPTEMBER 1976.
FRANKFURT / PARIS

The International Book Fair, Frankfurt.

This year's fair has been dedicated to Latin American literature and will culminate in a roundtable of writers who have been invited to come. Julio Cortázar and Mario Vargas Llosa are the stars of the "boom" here, although the bookstalls seem to be dominated by the blue covers of the German edition of Neruda's memoirs. Thiago de Melo, Eduardo Galeano, and I—along with Ernesto Cardenal, who is the star—are the children of the Peter Hammer Verlag of Wuppertal, a small but sound and spunky publishing house which manages to get its three children up on the stage where there has been an effort to accommodate the participating writers by quotas. It turns out that Peter Hammer is the publishing house with the most writers up there.

The roundtable conducted by Meyer-Classon is a failure, as are all roundtables where the audience expects Latin American writers to say something that creates a stir; all of them have something different and novel to say, but when all is said and done the speeches repeat one another.

Suddenly a counterpoint would seem to spring up between Cortázar and Vargas Llosa concerning the political question with reference to the writer, and other voices at the table support Cortázar's position, but I have the impression that it's nothing more than an *allegro* from up there; there is no fluidity in the debate because of the cumbersome translation which is finally eliminated altogether when it turns out that the great majority of those present speak Spanish. Given this, the terrible suspicion occurs to me—and I tell Galeano—that Latin American literature, still quite exotic as a cultural product, has a recurring public in Europe: a fraternity composed of university professors, language specialists, and our own exiles who are here occupying the front rows.

But the ritual has been carried out, and Hermann Schulz, our editor at Peter Hammer, is happy. In the courtyard of the fairground restaurant where they are going to offer us a farewell luncheon, I stand and chat with Julio while the first autumn gusts sweep leaves across the pavement, and beyond the windows the waiters in tuxedos, who would look like members of the country club in Nicaragua, are setting the tables. There is a photograph of that moment, someone walking around there takes it.

And I see Julio as if in another photo, dark tones and gray contrasts on the shiny paper. Rue de Savoie, the interior court with plants and flowerpots like an Argentine patio, a stairway with an iron handrail, a small

57

study with books, a living room crowded with guests where Ugné Karvelis plays the host at a reception for Luisa Valenzuela. In the photo, Julio would be in a corner, serious, tired, looking out over the heads of the guests.

Bored, he leaves, and we accompany him to say goodbye in the street, Roberto Armijo with his big astrakhan coat, the same one Rubén Darío pawned or sold in Paris and that turned up later in the hands of Gómez Carrillo, and Oscar Castillo who has come from afar in search of a lost love and has joined us to see Julio, Solentiname, Las Brisas, the river, the little plane. We remember.

Oscar embraces Julio emotionally, my favorite actor who never stops being Arturo Ui directed by Atahualpa del Chopo.

And the Frente Sandinista is still here, I answer Julio when he asks me about the struggle. It is here, growing like a rumor in the dark.

CENTRAL AMERICA,
ANTI-COMMUNISM, AND FOLKLORE
AT THE "SEVEN SEAS"

There is anti-communism and there is folklore.

Through the fairground telescope in the hands of the rich and powerful can be seen the dead remains of cultural misfortune, but with an insistent nudge in the ribs they urge you to admire their anti-communist décor as well; the bicycle wheel always spins to the right, and they offer you a walk through their enchanted forest, with its slimy waters and thorn trees, its swollen vegetation. The White Hand also holds newspapers with sonnets as page-fillers along with the crossword puzzle, and Maggie and Jiggs becomes the least of it—it is the phosphorescence of the emanations that counts; a winning acrostic dedicated to the queen of the Chalatenango festivals is awarded a prize of a thousand *colóns*, but nowadays the Dutriz brothers' telescope is loaned to you by Colonel d'Aubuisson, who is made up by Park Avenue image specialists, the death squads are seated in the Constituent Assembly of El Salvador because they have earned their seats by winning votes with colored balloons, pennants, and T-shirts—God, Homeland, Liberty is the emblem.

You have seen the black-shirted dwarfs of the Free Costa Rica movement parading through the forest; they are also the owners of the newspaper *La Nación* that prints vernacular Costa Rican legends on Sundays and worries about the purity of the language in page-long philological debates; and it's not just the Indians serving breakfast to the North American tourists in the hotels of Old Guatemala, disguised in sashes, sandals, straw hats, and all the other trappings that fate handed out to them, but also their villages that have been razed in order to liberate them from subversion and so their souls won't be won over by far-out ideas. Mario Sandoval Alarcón, seated in his office at the National Congress under the portrait of Castillo Armas, knows more about funeral rites than he does about expressionist painting.

The problem is that in the forest of swollen plants nothing ever changes, the air doesn't stir because the night air of Central America is subversive, the shadowy forest full of moans and full of slogans—property, fatherland, sacred spiritual values—the religion bequeathed to us by our elders speaks to you from the mouths of guns, the defense of democratic institutions is carried out in clandestine graveyards; in order to preserve family stability the roads of Jutiapa are filled with corpses, the cornfields of El Quiché are burning, and the Dragonflies are bombing the mountains in Perquin; the hand-cranked wells in Olancho are overflowing with murdered peasants because the great estate without borders continues to be the fatherland of the rich and powerful owners of the wheel and masters of the forest. And what are Somoza's guards of the Jean Kirkpatrick Task Force defending with their throat-cutting, razing, burning, if not western Christian democracy—here at the very edge of the forest, here where the forest ends?

The forest ends, there is a clearing in the purulent forest, and the bicycle wobbles, having lost the first spoke of its wheel. That is the source of the ill-will, the grudge; the Sandinista revolution represents for the rich and powerful of Central America an irruption, surprise, change, disturbance, annoyance, a cyst, an ingrown toenail, night terror. Nobody likes to be awakened suddenly from sleep—would you like it? Shackled dreams, serenity under chain and padlock suddenly shattered. And the rich and powerful who are so primitive as to offer the telescope with a thousand alarmed gestures so you can see what is happening in Nicaragua; the fairground loudspeakers blare: they are eating children over there, they roast them, fry them, quarter them, snatch them from their mothers' breasts in order to send them to Russia; they burn the saints, close the churches; religion is forbidden, it is forbidden to worship God, the Communist inferno, the totalitarian horror. The language of the caves is pathetic, its innocence is touching.

The rich and powerful were not prepared to see the world change; for them it was always the spurious tradition, forgetting, the continual exaltation of fear of change and the corresponding reward in inoffensive folklore that they have always cultivated, along with love for Central American union.

Folklore as the other inoffensive boundary of the Central American; anti-communism is the claw, folklore is the stump of the arm, popular tradition is expropriated in order to be sullied. In the telescope is the folkloric past that doesn't move; when it does move, it is subversive. Enough of appearances then; the only thing missing is the degradation, the forced appearance on stage of the conquered people with their holiday finery to participate in the great bloody kitsch spectacle. When you ask the rich and powerful about the people, they show you a hat with feathers, and now and then they hammer out a tune on the marimba with their iron drumsticks; but you already saw, in Monimbó, they taught the rich and powerful what masks are for.

In the clearing in the woods they made war wearing masks, the embalmed folklore was set in motion; the vernacular unsheathed its claws; the lifeless festival became a real festival, and we took popular tradition back from the rich and powerful.

That is why they're afraid.

JANUARY 1978. HAVANA

The restaurant in the Hotel Nacional. Miguel Barnet, Ugné Karvelis, and Julio, who is out in the sunlight this noon for the first time after a bout with pneumonia in a Havana hospital.

I was in Cuba as a judge in the Casa de las Américas competition, but mainly on business for the Frente Sandinista. There were intense months following the October 1977 offensive when the National Guard barracks in San Carlos on the San Juan River and in Masaya came under guerrilla fire, and fighting flared up with new intensity in the mountains to the north. The Group of Twelve had sprung up; Somoza was putting us on trial for sedition and had ordered the assassination of Pedro Joaquín Chamorro; the first barricades were going up in Managua; strikes were breaking out, and Monimbó was ablaze. The pieces of the insurrection were beginning to come together.

We were talking about all that in the golden semidarkness of the restaurant while we lunched, as if we were on the set of a Visconti film with a turn-of-the-century interior: curtains, tables, chairs, plates, pitchers illuminated by a very Darían light. And slices of guava, intensely red.

We were going to win the war; the conspiracy had now infiltrated the "boom." Cortázar enjoyed the story of our secret understanding with García Márquez, whom I had sought out in Bogotá months before to recruit him as our confidential agent in Miraflores Palace, Caracas. With the "boom," we were now able to enter presidential offices, and García Márquez already had a pseudonym among us.

Goodbye to Julio who was returning to Paris; and in the Hotel Hanabanilla in the Escambray Mountains where the jury was sequestered, Haydée Santamaría barricaded herself in her room like a naughty little girl, in complicity with me and Chico Buarque, piling up furniture against the door so her bodyguards couldn't get in. She had given them the slip in Havana, deliberately boarding the wrong plane and showing up alone in Cienfuegos.

I had finished my business for the FSLN in Havana and urgently needed to return, but here I was, trapped in the mountains, reading manuscripts with the rest of the jury. I urged Ernesto Cardenal, who was traveling with me, to explain to Haydée why we had to leave.

"Somoza is falling," he told her over breakfast in the hotel dining room. "We have to get back."

"You can't," she replied categorically. "If all the judges have to leave right away, there'll be no prize."

"There's a general strike," I told her, "and the Frente is going to attack Granada, attack Rivas. Things are speeding up."

She stared at us with a certain amused incredulity. If we were penned in here judging literary manuscripts, why should the FSLN have any need of us?

That night I won my freedom with a speech. All the judges were commemorating the anniversary of Martí's death in Tres Ríos with a public ceremony, and I recalled that on that same day, May 18, of that same year, 1895, Sandino was born, thus proving that the history of Latin America is a relay race. Haydée was moved, and she embraced me. I left the following morning, and Ernesto remained behind as a hostage.

And yes, during the first week of February, the FSLN surrounded the Guards in the Rivas barracks and took Rivas, and also surrounded the Guards in the Pólvora barracks and took Granada. That was enough to fan the flames that had started flickering in Monimbó: the Indians in colorful costumes who were rising up in Monimbó.

Panchito Gutiérrez had fallen in the attack on the Rivas barracks, and those were the days when we were entering the homestretch.

DAGUERREOTYPE

The day of the attack on Rivas, Panchito Gutiérrez, native of Diriamba and a combatant on the southern front, was in charge of the .50 caliber machine gun, the most noteworthy heavy weapon in FSLN hands until then. It had been cut out of the wing of an old Mustang fighter plane in the machine shop of Don Pepe Figueres's La Lucha Ranch. Panchito had carried the weapon on his back over the whole route the column, led by Father Gaspar García Laviana, had to cover, starting at midnight, to reach the outskirts of Rivas before dawn. He himself set up the weapon in the rear of a pickup parked two blocks away from the National Guard fortress.

Panchito was very serious-minded, like one of those schoolboys who sit in the first row; he didn't talk much and was stubborn. Once, in one of those badly furnished, nearly empty lodgings that were FSLN safe houses— transitory encampments set up in empty rooms where only a campfire was lacking to make you feel you were in the open air—Panchito found an ancient copy of *Playboy* that had been handled so much it was falling apart, and his only comment as he leafed indifferently through the pages was that such women didn't exist and never had existed.

They were tricks of capitalist propaganda: ordinary, everyday females whose photographs had been retouched and retouched to bring out that supernatural appearance. It was pointless to argue; nobody budged him from this position.

He himself set up the weapon in the back of the pickup, and nobody knows how many hours he had lugged it on his back through swamps, over hills, up rocky slopes. It was he who opened fire on the barracks, riding the gun like a bucking bronco, never letting go of it even when the barrel turned red hot, and the morning found him there, protecting the retreating column while the priest, Gaspar, was calling to him, and he was still firing in the clear dawn light.

They killed him, and he fell next to his gun. Even after he was dead, the Guards were afraid to approach the pickup because men like that didn't exist and never had existed.

CENTRAL AMERICA:
ENDGAME AT
THE "SEVEN SEAS"

What is Central American, therefore, is everything such as attitude, objective, cultural manifestation that because of birth injury, congenital blindness, a spirit of permanent surrender to the environment, or simple stupidity—either conscious or transmitted through provincial inheritance—loses the possibility of access to or connection with the universal and, instead of reflecting in dialectical terms any rupture or advance, improvement, discovery, progress, renewal, or innovation, simply accommodates itself to the vicious circling of the bicycle wheel.

One of its categories is, as we have already seen, meaningless vernacular art, the folkloric swindle that contributes to the stagnation of the popular dynamic in culture and is therefore indulgent about the inoffensive participation of tradition in everyday cultural acts: the same old design of the structure of domination and dependence imposed by the rich and powerful.

There are other categories of Central American: all sorts of academies, athenaeums, artistic societies, by means of which there is a constant celebration of the exhumation and reburial of inherited culture so that time itself in this rite only serves as a musty shroud that separates forms and experiences and continuously impoverishes and dries out the cultural corpse. Add to this ministerial publishing houses, schools of fine arts, and official conservatories, as well as literary supplements and cultural reviews.

But where the Central American excels is in the individual creative attitude, revealed not only in the work of art, but, even better, in behavior towards life and towards culture itself. In general, bad artists are incapable of understanding anything else, and neither do they understand the need for change in the world. They are happy with everything around them, including their own works of art, once they achieve official status—prizes, diplomas, titles, medals, and rewards—dispensed at the ritual celebrations that the rich and powerful hold in the dying forest.

Their lack of concern, or at least of curiosity, about the new goes hand in hand with their insensitivity toward the petrifaction of the system, and they quickly fall into the need to defend it openly, or timidly, as the best way of surviving without troubles or worries. The vital necessity for the renewal of knowledge, the awareness of new forms and the contribution to those new forms; active participation in the phenomenon of constant renewal of literature or painting is linked to the conscious necessity of the renewal of the world, and whoever doesn't want Central America to change could hardly want new art forms. Among us, the anachronism of cultural manifestations has a fatal correspondence with the anachronism of social structures. Therefore, the Central American culture to which we are referring is a celebration of that same past which the rich and powerful do not want to change.

But there is also the problem of badly understood or poorly assimilated modernity, which becomes another requisite of the Central American; it is not only the impossibility of accepting the world, but the impossibility of adequately understanding the changes, the new, so one ends up by laying novelty out in the coffin. Because of this, it isn't always easy to figure out the limits of this insensitivity toward the outside, where this sticky, swampy territory of the Central American begins when it is wrapped in that false modernity. Manlio is of the opinion that painting, with all its anachronistic and syncretic baggage, is the slipperiest terrain.

It is easiest to see the Central American in the purity of his acceptance of everything old, since this is an elemental plane on which a certain type of provincial art comes to be defended innocently as classical. Yes, we also have Central American classics: the *hai kai*, the sonnet, or assonant verses, continue to be classical: the *hai kai* as a false introduction of modernity which at one time was thought to fit the need for a magical, instantaneous expression when faced with tropical nature. That's very Central American, and so it became classic in the big homeland. The sonnet, and the half-verse generally, were an atemporal reaction to free verse, which hasn't yet been assimilated.

But let's return to the individual, to the lone artist who while walking through the swollen forest has chosen art as a form of personal expression for very diverse reasons, which, in the Central American context and its consequences, may include vocation and inspiration.

Vocation. It must be recognized that to take up art as a calling may be an act of legitimate choice—above all, if the choice is made in early youth and not as a later vocation, when there would be more grounds for suspicion. The environment, the impossibility, the conformity, the lack of understanding of the task in perspective—all of these corrupt this original impulse in Central America. The high walls are there, impassable; the forest becomes impenetrable, and the Central American artist begins, day by day, to carve his failure, to transform his original sensitivity into an ability to perceive the false and spurious as legitimate, to confound the loud with the new, to try to rescue old forms that in their time were new—far from Central American frontiers—and to incorporate into his closed universe formal experimentation per se, or provocative challenges to experimentation per se, or provocative challenges to established taste which are valid in other climates and whose transfer to a new environment renders them harmless from the outset; and how many times the abstract, and how many other times the realistic, the abstract as the best means of appearing modern and hiding the fact that one isn't a true artist, and the realistic as the most spurious way of assuming falsely a commitment to reality: poverty badly painted, the Indian head with the eyes bulging with terror or hunger. How very Central American.

And inspiration: inspiration as a permanent, continuing pretext; the fatal step from sensitivity to sentimentality, from sweetness to stickiness, from rigor to concession, from craftsmanship to shoddiness, from discipline to improvisation, from a critical sense to the merry clattering of the typewriter keys.

Extravagance, wastefulness, concession: one slides down that incline; from vocation one moves to inspiration, and we are stuffed with Central American art: the daily quota, the poem for the weekend supplement, the book that has to be finished for the contest, let's see if the masterpiece comes out, let's see if they give me the prize; and the high, impregnable walls that grow higher every day, surrounding the forest.

AFTER

JULIO CORTÁZAR'S TRIPS
TO NICARAGUA

Apart from his clandestine incursion into Solentiname in April 1976, we may say that Julio Cortázar's trips to Nicaragua following the revolutionary triumph of July 19, 1979, numbered five:

1. His first arrival with Carol Dunlop, in early November 1979, Paris/Martinique/Panama (where his passport was stolen), and then to Managua in Somoza's executive jet. His stay lasted until the end of November, and he attended the funeral of Carlos Fonseca, whose remains were brought from Zinica to Managua; he left after the nationalization of the mines.

2. After a lengthy period when he did not return (here I'd have to ask Tomás or Claribel, did he really not return?) he arrived in March 1982 for the meeting of the Permanent Committee of Intellectuals for the People's Sovereignty, together with Chico Buarque, Mariano Rodríguez, García Márquez, Matta.

3. Shortly after that he is in Nicaragua again for the third anniversary of the revolution; which we celebrate in Masaya in July 1982. He remains until the end of August or beginning of September. He returns unexpect-

edly to Paris with Carol, who is deathly ill. Remember San Francisco del Norte, El Velero.

4. Fourth trip. January 1983. He returns without Carol. The vigil in Bismuna, the Rubén Darío Order of Cultural Independence. Final visit to Solentiname.

5. Final trip, July 1983. Fourth anniversary of the revolution, with the main ceremony in León. Delivery of agrarian reform deeds in El Ostional. The mothers of Belén.

JULY, DAYS OF TRIUMPH, 1979. LEÓN

At midnight on July 17 we landed at Godoy, an airstrip on the outskirts of León, used for crop-dusting planes. A flight of nearly two hours from San José, flying over the ocean, following the coastline from afar. Wartime ingenuity had provided night lights for the small strip: two rows of yellow lights with a red arrow at the head, almost sophistication. The odor of insecticide on landing, shadows in fatigue outfits, weapons, vehicles of all sorts, bear hugs. There are two light planes: Ernesto Cardenal and I came in the one that landed first, together with Juan Ignacio Gutiérrez, the Junta's medical doctor. Robelo and Doña Violeta arrived in the second.

We awaken in a house abandoned by its cotton-planting owner, who has gone to spend the war in Miami with his family. Daniel, Tomás, and Jaime are already installed here. It is a quiet residential neighborhood on the road to the Poneloya beach resort. One might almost have heard the sprinklers scattering water over the grass in a fine transparent shower—if there had been any water. There is no electricity either, but that will be turned back on later. We have slept on mattresses put down on the floor, with no sheets. It is hot, as Juan Ignacio vaccinates us against tetanus.

We meet in the patio with Dora María very early, sitting in a circle in big Leonese rocking chairs. Pale and self-confident, she smiles, smokes, nods. Dora María Téllez, military and political chief of the stronghold of León, twenty-five years old. She was the heroine of the seizure of the National Palace on August 22 of the previous year; afterwards she led the taking of the city, the attack on the departmental command of the National Guard from where General Everst (Volcano) had to flee, shielding himself with prisoners, women, and children, to the Fortín, an old military fortress on the outskirts of the city, only to be expelled from there once more by the rebelling people.

Now León is completely liberated and is the seat of the revolutionary government; the Junta is already in the city. Dora María explains to us that to defend León it is necessary to advance against the neighboring towns located along the road to Managua; no circular trenches, but an active defense, the conquest of new positions, new strongholds. And that same day, Sandinista columns are fighting in La Paz Centro, in Puerto Somoza, and are advancing toward Nagarote. The enemy doesn't realize that today León has no more than fifty combat troops equipped with assault rifles; all the forces are fighting in the attack and some have been shifted to the rear where Somoza's army still has organized units in Somotillo, El

Sauce, Achuapa. But Dora María smokes, smiles, nods, and in any event the city seems to be full of guerrillas armed to the teeth. There are uniformed kids everywhere with all sorts of weapons; the visual magic of the insurrection.

We leave for León before midday. The proclamation of the city as provisional capital will be made in a public ceremony in the University auditorium; we're talking about July 18, 1979. The caravan is being organized with cars, jeeps, pickup trucks, with guerrillas crowded into each vehicle: everybody wants to be in the caravan that crosses the city along the Calle Real. There are armed reservists and barricades at each corner.

The University auditorium, with its glass doors closed, that is now filled with journalists, photographers, television cameras. The members of the Junta, together with Tomás and Jaime, occupy the high carved chairs beneath the portraits of the founders, priests and academicians, which were there in the distant days of the student riots and assemblies, the demonstrations which from this hall—where the chandeliers were always shining even in daytime—sallied forth into the streets to confront the Guard. There is the same bloodied flag from July 23, 1959, and you can almost hear the voices, the haranguing of Fernando Gordillo, the applause, and the cries of "Death to Somoza!" "Down with the dictatorship!" The students crowding the doorways, carrying flags. It's enough to make you weep, if there were time enough, Julio.

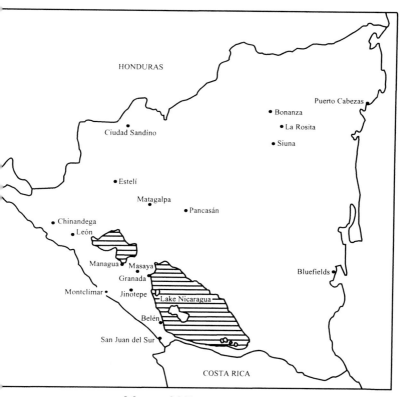

Map of Nicaragua

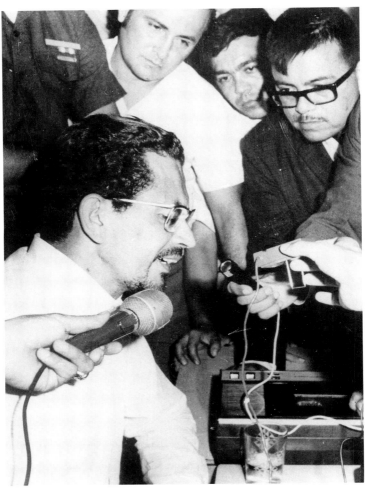

Carlos Fonseca

Julio Cortázar with Claribel Alegría and Michaele Najlis during the Bismuna vigil

Roque Dalton

Lizando Chávez, Julio, Gabriel García Márquez, Rogelio Sinán and Rosario Murillo. Lecture at the Fernando Gordillo center, headquarters for the Sandinista Association of Cultural Workers

Ernesto Cardenal, Julio Cortázar and Julio Valle Castillo during a lecture in the Edgar Munguia Theater

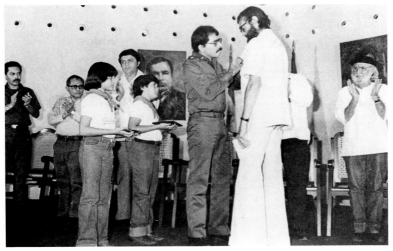

Julio receiving the Rubén Darío Order of Cultural Independence from
Daniel Ortega

Julio with Ernesto Cardenal

Julio and Carol

Sergio Ramírez talking with the mother of Rigoberto Cruz (Pablo Ubeda), hero of Pancasán

Gaspar García Laviana

Julio Cortázar

And once again I'm in the same hall with Jaime where we taught the students about the "boom," about the new novel, about *Hopscotch*, where we heard the news that Che had fallen; we've returned to the University. And when we go out on the street, the crowd follows us; everybody is rushing to the middle of the street this noonday in León, the revolutionary procession, enthusiasm, anxiety, happiness, hope, lightning meetings, street-corner speeches, press interviews under a sky that is beginning to cloud over; now from the fire station we walk toward the Ruiz Ayestas auditorium of the University where they are keeping vigil over Fanor Urroz, the second in command at León, who fell in the attack on La Paz Centro. The red and black banners so near, the texture of the cloth they are made of so real, the hands that hold them up in the crowd so firm, they'd grasp a rifle the same way; the humble strength of the poor who are walking in the middle of the street.

We leave with the caravan for Chichigalpa where they're holding a popular gathering at the baseball stadium; it must be four in the afternoon. Marimbas, sky rockets, songs: "Power to the workers!" the crowd chants, and *María Rural* comes from every throat. The Pancasán group is there with the song Arlen Siu composed, a song that clearly evokes those days; a song like no other.

And the caravan moving again toward Chinandega at nightfall. Guerrilla columns arrive along side roads and gather in front of the Hotel Cosigüina which is closed and which we order reopened to accommodate the troops. Barefoot, wearing tattered boots and torn clothing, the combatants cross the streets in the darkness, and in the darkness you hear the clang of their weapons against the pavement. Jaime talks to them, Daniel talks to them; I've already talked to them; and they listen to us silently in the liberated night while the sea breeze brings us a distant scent of rain.

And back at the house that night, I am conversing with Omar Cabezas, whom I see for the first time in my life, both of us sitting on the floor. El Moro is speaking, tall, dark, corpulent, also sitting on the floor, a bullet graze red and raw above his eyebrow. After we returned from Chinandega, there was a skirmish with fleeing Guards near the crossroads between Chinandega and Corinto. A skirmish, hidden Guards; it's midnight and the voices are dreamlike.

And the 19th of July dawns. I come out of the room because I hear Dora's voice. Polo Rivas has reached the Open with the light tanks captured from the Guard; we're in the outskirts of Managua, and the Western Front controls the entire highway. Breakfast time so rushed in the kitchen, once again eating on your feet your ration of beans and rice, you begin to realize that today is the day; such days don't exist until they are over, but today is the day; the music of *The Women of Cuá* on all the stations of the little black radio that blares on top of the pantry tiles; *The Guerrillas' Tomb*, that music is dominating the air waves; Radio Tiempo of Managua at the head of a chain of stations is like a gentle magic, a cordial but firm little touch to shake your incredulity, open your eyes; listen, you can walk and you don't feel the floor, a mattress of clouds on the floor; today is the day, and as if it were a baseball game, the announcer is enthusiastically describing the arrival of the first trucks, bulging with Guerrillas; they are entering Managua; you hear the shouts, the slogans; the columns are arriving from Carazo along the southern highway; they're also coming along the Masaya highway; the caravan has reached the eastern highway; the light tanks, draped in red and black, of Polo Rivas's armored unit, are already in Nejapa and the Northern Front is coming down from Sébaco, merging with troops from Estelí and Matagalpa; the advance guard of the Northeastern Front, who are coming from Juigalpa and Boaco, are already in San Benito, joining the forces coming down from Matagalpa and Estelí, and they've opened the gates of the Model Prison in Tipitapa; they've taken the airport. Today is the day.

And everyone in the house is suddenly crowded around the television screen where the image of Sandino repeatedly takes off his hat and puts it back on, again and again, to the chords of the Sandinista hymn; and that was the best proof that this day really existed: Sandino taking off his hat and putting it back on this morning of July 19, 1979, on all the television screens. Who was going to deny that we had triumphed and from now on there would always be a 19th of July, 1979.

It was decided that we wouldn't go to Managua until the following day. But Henry Ruiz insisted from the airport, where his forces were already camped with those of Bayardo and Luis, that it was necessary that the Junta speak with Bowdler. Bowdler, Mister Bowdler, Henry's voice repeated as he spoke with Daniel over the radio. "Office," which was Managua, calling "Workshop," which was León; the portable "Office" radio had been moved to the airport, now headquarters of the National Directorate.

Mister Bowdler was already in Managua, and he kept on pestering us about the ceremony of transmission of power that we had accepted in San José before Urcuyo did us the great favor of refusing to resign. The Yankees kept insisting on an "orderly transition," even though Urcuyo had already fled the country, and what kind of orderly transition when, since early morning, the guerrillas of the Western Front had been soaping themselves in Somoza's bathtub in the bunker? We had to talk to Bowdler, to the Chancellors from the Andean Pact countries; we had to manage things. Manage things, Julio, brother; how much we've learned from that one little word.

And Daniel told me it couldn't be helped; I had to go. And that afternoon of July 19, 1979, I flew to Managua; I had become an expert on Bowdler after so many days of negotiation in Panama and in Costa Rica. Modesto Rojas piloted the "Aerocommander" that serenely followed a course along the edge of the lake; the immense plains to the south lost in the afternoon haze, the first rocky elevations of the Managua range, the high, hard crags and their indistinct ribs, and towards the north the black mass of Momotombo and the small waves of the lake rippling, and noiselessly, almost motionlessly, licking at the shoreline.

And the poor scattered lights of Managua in the dusk. I saw it then from the air, standing among ruins, beautiful amidst the wasteland, poor as the arms it fought with, rich as the blood of its children. Managua, this was Managua.

THE STRATEGY OF THE EAGLE

1. *The eagle is bald because he hasn't a single stupid hair*

Much has been said about the contradiction between the Latin American being and the European (Europe in any case as the exquisitely remote, which is adoptable or worthy of rejection), and these days the same holds true for the position of this same being confronted with the Oriental/Occidental contradiction (more precisely and in terms of semantic usage, the East/West contradiction), but not enough has been said (as it certainly should have been) about the US/Latin America contradiction, which is much more important because here the being definitively risks an end to being.

In the days of *Hopscotch*, the proposition of that black volume with magical properties was directed more towards the fixation with and consequent resolution of the European/Latin American contradiction; it occurred to you then that, because the book opened ontologically towards both worlds, Cortázar remained on the right side, thanks to certain worrisome antecedents: he was born, although accidentally, in Belgium; Paris was his adoptive fatherland, and what was even worse, he spoke Spanish with fat "r's." After all, the Latin American intellectual, suckled in these lands where milk is scarce, had only to embark one day, cross the Atlantic, and get off in Marseilles or Barcelona for the whole thing to turn into nothing less than a one-way trip. Latin America's role was to export desserts, as Manlio Argueta expressed it so well in midday conversations at the Seven Seas in San Salvador—cacao, bananas, coffee—and Chateaubriand on the way back with a few snatches of warmth/local color staining one's overcoat.

But *Hopscotch* was not a novel of Paris. Our Latin American writers (and this is one of the unequivocal marks of Latin American provincialism) fixed on the end of the nineteenth century for the action of their stories and novels set in Paris—where none of them had ever been—and not only that, but they sent their books to French publishers to be printed in Spanish, all of which goes to show that there existed an irrepressible artificial nostalgia that was, by extension an impotence or an impossibility.

Hopscotch was already a Latin American novel, of this side; not the exquisitely remote, but the remote as counterpoint. Oliveira and Talita returned, came back to this side, and Europe remained on that side. The thing is that, as far as the consequences are important, Cortázar also remained on this side, and the Seine, like any green and turbulent San Juan river, finally flowed into the Great Lake of Nicaragua.

If you assume, incorrectly, that the dialectical confrontation is between two old continents, the one on this side and the other on that, the expertise of good taste and love of refinement will undoubtedly oblige you to choose that one (the patina is more ancient and less republican; the palaces are truly old and not copied from turn-of-the-century architectural catalogs, and the ruins are Greco-Roman and not indigenous). But if you assume, more correctly, that the dialectical opposition is between the old and the new, and if as a detonator of the new you have the permanent possibility of revolution, change, and renewal, all this Triptolemic labor Rubén talked about (Triptolemus undertaking agrarian reform in the name of Demeter), then you must recognize that the true choice is to be found on this side.

You must take into account, in this matter of dialectical renewal, that it does have to do with the Latin American being when it is a matter of conscious choice, and whoever isn't able to discern that will die in the claws of unfulfilled nostalgia and will end up wrapped in the shroud of impossibility. One can grow old speaking Spanish with fat "r's" without being Cortázar.

Many Latin American intellectuals have been incapable of understanding the dilemma, of understanding how crucial this choice becomes, how much more important than that other worn-out choice between East and West. This or that, which as can be seen, tries to implicate you in a fatal selection, the trap being set by those who, with not very good intentions, force you to choose.

The East/West confrontation is a very European philosophical category and a very North American political category, by which I mean that for the Latin American being it is not a category at all.

Obviously, western Europe has a frontier with eastern Europe, and there are concrete contradictory interests at stake all along that border, on this side of which are commonly situated a series of values referred to as western and which we Latin Americans, of course, do not reject. We also clearly understand that the medium-range missiles the US has placed all along that border are there to defend the Europeans in the scenario of a limited nuclear war in which President Reagan himself has said there would be no reason to endanger North American cities. We suspect that in some way that swarm of missiles has also been set in place to defend that catalog of western values: pluralism, parliamentary democracy, freedom of speech, respect for the individual—values in which the ideologues of the New Right, who now light their campfires in the caverns of the White House, claim to be interested.

Although we must never forget that out of this conglomeration of values we in Latin America have only received the leftovers, our contradiction is not with the west, nor could it be, but with its great military defender, Reagan himself, who brandishes his nuclear shield to fight for the west and incidentally tries to crush us in Nicaragua in the name of western values.

From there we pass to the third of these contradictions, that between Latin America and the United States, which is being played out in a renewed and corrosive way as a head-on confrontation with no quarter asked or given ever since the triumph of the Sandinista revolution in 1979. Think of the irony of the fact that a popular revolution proclaiming its national independence in the face of the Colossus of the North—so-called with a certain fear and affection by some, and with manifest hatred by others—is taking place in a small, weak, impoverished country with no economic resources, no oil, no industrial development, with an enormous mass of peasants who are only now attaining a modern form of productive organization, with a travesty of a bourgeoisie that has grown servile in its spurious carnal contact with the empire. And think of the empire with the capability of extending its strategic frontiers close to us at its own convenience and whim: Nicaragua bounded on the north by the United States, on the south by the United States, on the east by the Nimitz and its accompanying fleet, on the west by the Eisenhower and its accompanying fleet, and overhead by the R-4 and U-2 spy planes. What luck that our subsoil is still free of the good neighbor's presence!

And just think that the only thing this country has is its will, its clear gaze, its historic intransigence, its people in arms, its political skill. It is ironic, I have said, because probably a revolution like this, with such a will, such decisiveness and such invincible courage, would have been more comfortable for Latin America had it taken place in a large country of the Southern Cone so the Yankees would be frantically trying to extend their portable frontiers that far, and perhaps they wouldn't find it all that easy to obtain a Honduras in those latitudes.

But the Sandinista revolution is not an accident of history, much less one of destiny's ironies. We didn't win it in a raffle; we made it, and we continue to make it. What disproportion between the Colossus of the North and ourselves! I bring this up simply because it shouldn't be forgotten—as it frequently is—that this isn't the War of the Galaxies nor is it a confrontation between two superpowers.

The dilemma, therefore, is highly complex. We can't tow Nicaragua away from the coasts of Central America and drop anchor calmly off the port of Odessa; we have to defend ourselves from Reagan while remaining part of the west and located in the backyard of the defender of the west; we have to try to establish and really consolidate—and not in the abstract—what the west has considered, ever since the century of the Enlightenment, to be its best values. We have to achieve a type of democracy that corresponds to our tradition of struggle for independence and to define our historic profile within a geographic neighborhood that is full of risks and which we didn't choose. A democracy that functions and restores to the word "democracy" its original, practical meaning (the fact that it has been necessary to add to the word "democracy" the qualifier "popular" merely demonstrates the inefficacy and erosion of the term to express its meaning of "power of the people" in western terms) without having to blush about preaching democracy according to classical canons while practicing totalitarianism, which has never stopped being western and which definitely does exist in Latin America; Central America is its great kingdom—a kingdom of the constant violation of as many western values as you can think of. Western and Christian values, and without any of this ever disturbing the United States. Why should it be disturbed?

JULY/SEPTEMBER 1979.
FREE NICARAGUA

These are the days when the ground still trembles, shaken by the expanding waves; you can feel the revolution underfoot. When we left the Central Bank auditorium on July 27, 1979, after announcing the nationalization of the banks, the ground went on trembling; the huge subterranean collapses continued; mountains split apart; bubbling lava flowed down in incandescent cascades; the landscape altered abruptly under the weight of the cataclysm.

The days we lived crowded together in Managua's Hotel Intercontinental among legions of newspapermen; Daniel and I occupied adjacent cells on the third floor; we only came back to the rooms for a few hours of restless sleep and to keep talking, discussing, planning, and then we'd go out on the street again to try to bring order into the disorderly world, to channel the streams of bubbling lava, shape the seething magma; seated day and night at the huge conference table in Government House, camped there from day to night to dawn to receive ambassadors' credentials, visionaries with projects to change the course of the rivers and divert the waters of Lake Cocibolca into

Lake Xolotlán, thus converting Managua into a seaport on both the Atlantic and the Pacific; petitions for street lighting from mayors of the most humble hamlets along the Honduran border; peasants who knew of oil deposits in their regions, reports of hidden treasures left behind when the guards fled; secret tunnels of the Somoza security service clogged with corpses; the treasure vault of old Somoza's wife in a Managua cellar, heaped with gifts she had never opened; the true location of Sandino's grave; mothers of heroes with photos of their disappeared children; and the dethroned princes of private enterprise with their interminable lists of grievances.

These are the days when we went in search of the country, trying to devour it: long hikes, caravans, public ceremonies, swearings in, drinking in the fields, drinking with the people, looks, gestures, laughs, worries; intoxication with the country that was now ours; change it, turn it around, discover the seams of injustice and suffering, with eagerness, with sharp nostalgia; the urge to make and unmake; a permanent lump in the throat; feelings alert; love so great and anger so deep that feeling became a way of life. And also, learning to speak. I had been a champion orator, trained in university assemblies, but not until now did I have to learn how to really speak. Forget rhetoric; here what the people want is the truth; you have to look them in the eye and tell them what we are doing and where we are headed.

Macuelizo, Limay, Yalí, Palacaguina. The blades of the old, beat-up "Sikorski" lash the cold air while the hazy solitude of the hard blue mountains touches us from the open door of the helicopter that creaks with the wind. We pass like a shadow above the pines that rest in quiet obscurity in the hollows, among the crests of the bald, bulging mountains; abysses that open far and near, and suddenly once more above the distant chasm, after flying nearly level with the yellow pastures peacefully undulating, we are lost over Concordia, Yalí, Condega, landing in distant, astonished villages; unknown settlements, cows, horses that go galloping off; women come carrying their children to surround the helicopter.

The little blond girl, in these mountains of blond peasants, marks the rhythm with a bare foot while she sings without meeting our eyes; her head is bent to better string together the memory of her song which tells of Sandino's war, and the combatants in damp uniforms surrounding her in heavy silence while the nearly blind old soldier of Sandino's army, who has come on horseback to tell us his stories of ambushes and battles— waving his hat and stamping the wooden floor—is crying wordlessly now as he listens to the song from those days.

And when we landed, they asked us if we had come down because we saw the flag. They had hung a flag in a treetop so it might be seen from the air, because they had heard that it was necessary to put up a flag as a signal for the revolution to come and visit them in those lonely areas.

A school, a health center, a school; we lay the cornerstone, we have the wood; a school, here is the impulse to build it; a shipment of lime, a load of sand; we have the land; a school, you should see how beautiful the children are; a school, a health center, a road; a blessing of children; the school, a loveliness of children, once upon a time there was a school teacher; will he come back?

A school, a school, a school.

OCTOBER 1979. CASARES

Now Julio Cortázar is here. I see him in the sunlight at the beach resort of Casares, on the Pacific coast of Nicaragua, sitting in a rustic beach rocking chair in the little patio facing the foaming, tossing sea breaking against black rocks. The green and red almond leaves don't give enough shade, but nobody suggests taking refuge in the old wooden house with its cross-hatched skylights like a birdcage.

We have just been in San Marcos, the birthplace of old Somoza, where the new municipal council was sworn in. We've already mentioned that this is the time of administering oaths, of caravans, of public ceremonies that could last an entire day (in, August 1979, I attended one with Bayardo, celebrated in the humble baseball stadium: it lasted from ten in the morning until four in the afternoon, open air mass included), and afterward we wound up here with Tomás and Claribel.

In the patio where the shadows of the almond trees move over the hard sand as if over the surface of boiling water, we hear the interminable tale of a fourteen-year-old boy about his combat experiences. Julio listens amazed, absorbed, gazing thoughtfully at the boy and turning to look at us with a nod of affirmative disdain: the power of incredulity and the conscious fascination of credulity which becomes the legitimate key to astonishment. And don't tigers also wander through empty rooms?

Next door, the summer home of one of Somoza's colonels has been turned into a community center; fishermen's wives take us to see their craft exhibition: handwork made of seashells, driftwood, coral, and cocoa fiber. They give us something as a souvenir while we stand around the big table, the only piece of furniture in the sacked house. The women speak of the revolution with domestic familiarity.

Carol Dunlop, moving from one side to the other, takes photographs. In some closed cabinet, folder, or drawer, in France or Canada, these must still exist. There is a midday sun at that moment, a dazzle of sea and smiles, the embraces of the women, all together in that embrace. That instant exists.

CORTÁZAR AMONG US

2. *Feathering the eagle.*

Julio Cortázar knew how to resolve that first intellectual dilemma about the man of two worlds, the choice between a European world and a Latin American one. He chose to return; his was not a voyage of no return, despite the fact that he is buried in Montparnasse. And he well knew the other two dilemmas: that of East and West, proposed as a trap; and the latter—the one that refers to the United States—he resolved in the concrete fact of Nicaragua.

There are returns, but also a single moment of returning. And the dialectical relief map of the coast where he had to land was Nicaragua (we aren't going to speak here of the rich relationship of Julio Cortázar with Cuba, which is also confronting the United States). All of this is very important to émigré intellectuals before whose eyes there will always exist the possibility of spotting a stormy stretch of coast awaiting them, a revolution emerging, a poor people in a wasteland who will display their hopes among their rags; any port on the relief map of the coast of Latin America that extends across the living distance of history; the future, of which Rubén spoke, that is silent and waits.

With Cortázar ended the myth of the man of two worlds who only knows how to waver on the edge of the abyss and winds up being neither on that side nor this, with the risk that, after so much fastidiousness, meditation, parsimony, he will end up going over, cartridge belt and all, to the side of the Colossus of the North—the good neighbor or silver-toothed buffalo, however you want it—which is when the choice really has tragic consequences.

One can grow old harmlessly in Paris, drying out, shriveling up; or one can do the same in Mexico atop a pyramid as a simple subjective observer of the world, which harms nobody either; but to actively go over to the side of the Colossus and become a part of its ideological conspiracies, its monumental machinations, and its formidable brainwashing is going too far. However competent a poet one has learned to be, it is a tragedy to wind up playing four-hand piano duets with Reagan and swearing that in Nicaragua the red tide of international communism is suffocating the Latin American being, the individual, under the most vile Bolshevik totalitarianism. When someone lends his signature and his prestige to that sort of tawdry scheme simply to remain at peace with the devil and his American dream, one can't help but accept the fact that here in Nicaragua we fry babies in oil. And then, what good are all your efforts at poetic abstraction, all your complications of verbal discipline, all your enigmatic contributions to the language?

The individual, the freedom of the individual; the being, the vital space of being. Some Latin American intellectuals, in order to be no less liberal than certain intellectuals in the United States and in order not to clash with the spirit of the Alliance for Progress—inasmuch as Kennedy admired Robert Frost and invited Pablo Casals to play at the White House—allowed themselves a modest space of critical conduct with respect to the imperial policies of the United States as long as the extreme aggressiveness of the New Right—entrenched in the same White House where Casals' cello was once heard—didn't close off that space. But when the eagle starts constantly flapping his wings, showing his claws, and covering everything with his ominous shadow, one must beat a retreat, leaving all excuses—and there are all too many excuses—behind. It is then that the concept of freedom, or the word "freedom," becomes as elastic as Adams chewing gum, and one must defend it, because otherwise Sandinista totalitarianism will eat it alive.

Freedom in such a case becomes the most obscene of fetishes; nothing can be sacrificed that opposes freedom; the individual brought up on intellectual abstractions cannot lose his vital living space; revolutions without that sort of freedom cannot be justified. And there's no need to come and ask us Sandinistas what we think about freedom; they take it for granted that, being revolutionaries, we are its sworn enemies. And what is even more terrible, we have guns.

If they were to ask us, our initial response would be that "the individual" and "freedom" have for the most part been no more than verbal abstractions in the history of Latin America; and terms of comparison are scarce, or deceitful, in attempting to measure the amount of freedom in a country shaken by a revolution that is also defending itself to the death against the power of a United States that is not trying to destroy us with mere theoretical intransigencies, but with systematic acts of terror, manipulation, blackmail, desolation, death. It is in this context that the individual in Nicaragua is respected in his true individuality, not as the object of vague theories but in the concrete practice of his liberated existence: freedom, not as an issue to be elucidated between individuals, but with respect to the whole vast and diverse conglomeration of men and women who struggle to be free every day in the face of the ferocious hatred of the Moonies and the illuminati of Manifest Destiny— McFarlane, Kirkpatrick, and Reich—who, to the despair of freedom lovers of the highest order, prefer supermarket Muzak to Casals.

Conceptual abstractions turn out to be echoes of abstraction itself, when one tries to establish a field of action or combat in real, precise terms for these ideas that are the offspring of docility and fear; because if the Sandinista revolution does have something to offer, it is a new, concrete historic profile that is not static.

The least that could be done—were the eagle not watching them so closely and with such shrill screams—would be to accept the experimental sense that freedom has in a revolution where they don't want to leave us so much as fingernails to defend ourselves with. They might at least give it the benefit of time, permitting it to progress in its consolidation and development. But, under the ideological terror of the Reagan era, the easiest thing has been to accept the idea that, fatally and infallibly, the Sandinistas are headed toward a seamless totalitarianism, and that only the *deus ex machina,* thundering Reagan himself, can reestablish the power balance and correct the proportion of the lost idea of freedom.

In Nicaragua, freedom has been born as a new phenomenon for thousands who don't read the *Washington Times,* who don't know that the magazine *Vuelta* exists, and who also don't have access to the Congressional Record. Where the discussions center on whether they should strangle us today and get it over with or whether it should be death on the installment plan with the right to a last wish before the execution. To allow the very western right of freedom of speech to vegetable sellers, porters, rural teachers who teach without blackboards, militiamen who plow with rifles slung over their shoulders, who could easily pick up a microphone and explain to you with astonishing lucidity just what freedom means among us. That is, if anyone asked them.

OCTOBER 1979. SIUNA

The day of the nationalization of the mines. In keeping with the dramatics of the unexpected with which we did things in those days, I telephone Julio and invite him to come to Siuna with Daniel and me the following day. The motive: historic; you'll know tomorrow.

The "Aviocar," a military transport plane, flies toward the Atlantic loaded with leaders, escorts, journalists, alongside an old "DC-3," also packed. Tree stumps and the solitude of decapitated trees between the wisps of fog, forests once leafy and now barren. In my briefcase travels the decree of nationalization of the mines.

"The decision is up to you," the Yankee representative of the mining companies would tell me three days later as we sat at the huge conference table in Government House, once again in Managua. "The decision is up to you, but you are making a mistake; without us you'll never be able to manage those mines."

Now we had landed and were waiting in the sun for the miners to come out of the shafts and gather next to the building where they collect the tailings and carry them to the old nineteenth-century crushing mill which was about to be expropriated along with all that history.

Whatever happened, we could never have forgotten the mines.

There in the humid heat of Siuna, next to the shed that serves as the airport office (the airport is a dark brown strip, next to which horses are tearing up mouthfuls of dry grass). Carol has taken a picture of me while I chat with a couple of elderly blacks. The miners have begun to arrive, gathering around Daniel. The mine whistle keeps on blowing. Years of misery and ruin, of wicked exploitation, of abandonment, degradation, of ridicule and mockery; mark those words. They do not exaggerate.

It was during those months that I began to collect the items that will one day become our Museum of Horrors: photographs, letters, documents, checks, receipts, dossiers, the intimate history of the carnal relationship between Somocism and imperialism. Among these items are examples of the work records of miners—Zambos, Miskitos, Criollos, Ladinos—crushed in the tunnels, sent back to their hovels with tuberculosis, cheated of their pay, fired as useless when X-rays (which were only taken for that reason) revealed the presence of silicosis. But to die inside the mine was also a violation of the labor contract and cause for discharge. Yes, that's right. Here is one of the items for the museum:

> *La Luz Mines, Limited*
> *Record of Employment*
> *Name: José Villarreina Hernández*

You can see the face of José Villarreina Hernández progress from the freshness of his peasant youth, in the photos stapled successively into his work folder, to his premature decrepitude *Date of birth:* 12 April 1928. He looks at the camera hopefully in this first photo, his hair brushed back in two dark wings. *Date of contract:* 18/4/52, by now the wrinkles of his martyrdom begin to look like knife slashes on his forehead. The last photo was taken in 1973.

He started as a shaft operator at 1.25 córdobas per hour, he became a road-gang operator at 1.60, a driller helper at 1.80, a shaft machinist at 2.50, and a miner at 2.75. Twenty-five years in the pits to reach 2.75, and his right thumb print at the bottom of each page of his dossier throughout those twenty-five years, because he didn't know how to sign his name. *Beneficiary in the event of death:* Elsa Obando (Condega). *Names of children:* Blanca Villarreina (this name is crossed out), Agustín Villarreina, María Villarreina. Why the hell did the mine want the names of his children?

Event of death: He died at 1:30 p.m. on July 13, 1979. *Was there carelessness on the part of the deceased?* Yes. *In what way?* He stuck his head into the path of a bucket without checking to make sure that the bucket was stationary. *Describe how the accident occurred:* At that moment the bucket went past and struck him on the head. *Death:* Instantaneous.

ROSARIO MINING OF
NICARAGUA, INC.
DISCHARGE

Rosita, July 13, 1979
Mr. José Villarreina
This letter.

In conformity with paragraph 4, article 115 of articles (18) and (119) of the Labor Code, you are discharged as an employee of this enterprise, the causes of said legal discharge being known to you, inasmuch as you have violated your labor contract in the following manner.

On the discharge slip, the name of José Villarreina is filled in by hand; the date he was fired, July 13, 1979, when he was already dead, has also been filled in by hand, the articles violated by the dead José Villarreina filled in by hand. And at the bottom of the page, also handwritten so there should be no doubt: *Reason for discharge: death of the worker.*

On the thirteenth of July 1979, what were we doing? At the noon hour when José Villarreina entered the tunnel for the last time in his life, where was Dora María, where was Zorro? And Elías Noguera, and Omar, and Julio

106

Ramos? We had already taken León, the red and black banner was flying above the Fortín, and in Matagalpa the Guard had finally surrendered in the cathedral, and Estelí and Jinotepe, and Diriamba; we had Masaya. "Office" calling "Workshop," "Rocío" here, "Rocío" calling "Chaparral," gunfire could be heard all over Nicaragua and José Villarreina there in the darkness of the tunnel, and the mine kept on producing gold and the gold kept on leaving by the Prinzapolka River to the Atlantic; the savage foremen were still in the mouths of the tunnels, and the Yankee bookkeepers with their ledgers open on their desks; the National Guard detachment stationed in Siuna still hadn't deserted, and José Villarreina could still be fired after he was dead. So many deaths during those years of conjugal collusion:

The above check in full payment of items hereon General Anastasio Somoza García
Excmo. Presidente de la Rpca de Nic
To pay subsidy tax of $10.00 per each kilo of gold shipped by La Luz Mines Limited from July 1, 1951 to December 31, 1951: $10,735.00.
Sus attos y SS:
T.N. Slaughter
Manager

Imperishable items for the Museum of Horrors from that scandalous concubinage. It was certainly amusing that the head butcher of the mine should be named

Slaughter, and with what finesse he remitted the agreed-upon bribe for his dirty business to old Somoza.

Thievery, hunger, misery, ridicule, deceit, silicosis: national sovereignty meant balls to them. We might have overlooked anything else in those days, anything but the mines; that was an act of rage. Omar Cabezas solemnly read the decree of expropriation, and Daniel's voice echoed in the sticky heat of Siuna above the heads, above the yellow helmets of the miners, crowded together and silent, and suddenly they started applauding and kept on applauding. Did Carlos Mejía sing? Did we sleep in Siuna at the end of that historic day?

Daniel traveled on to Puerto Cabezas in the "Aviocar," now more heavily loaded than ever, and I returned with Julio and Carol to Managua. There was a broom traveling with us in the airplane, leaning against the cabin wall. Julio passed me this note scrawled on a scrap of Kraft paper torn from an airsickness bag:

> *Sergio, I'll always be grateful for a trip when you gave me a unique opportunity: to see a broom in an airplane.*
> *—Julio*
> *P.S. The broom, in case you don't believe me, is two meters from where Carol is sitting.*

The broom came back with us. Apart from its surrealistic presence, the fact of the matter is that there was still a lot that needed sweeping out.

MARCH 1982. MANAGUA

There are two trips by Julio Cortázar to Nicaragua in this period, very close together, because he would return for the fourth anniversary of the revolution in July. Now he's here for the First Reunion of the Permanent Committee of Intellectuals for the Sovereignty of the Peoples of Our America, which was inaugurated on March 4 in Managua at the César Augusto Silva Convention Center, where Julio was also to receive our Rubén Darío medal in 1983 (the convention center used to be the country club of the shipwrecked: its auditorium was the ballroom, and the green golf course is still there).

Managua was a cultural capital in the month of March 1982, and the phrase was no less true for being a cliché: we opened an exhibition of Julio Leparc in the Rubén Darío Theater, with his *Modulations* hung on the walls that Doña Hope Somoza had erected so she could hear *Granada* with good acoustics; we had roundtables, readings, symposia with Julio, García Márquez, Rogelio Sinán; Roberto Matta bought brightly colored hats in the Masaya market, and the crayon drawing *Somoza and Gomorra* that he gave my wife dates from that time. And Chico Buarque was there, as was Antonio Skármeta, who had just spent several months in León with Peter Lilienthal, filming *The Insurrection,* and now, yes, we had finally closed the triangle.

It was then that Julio pulled out from the Cortázar shelf of my books the old, much-thumbed copy of *Hopscotch* for one of his readings under the stars in the Sandinista night for aspiring writers, young artists, university students, and a multitude of soldiers sprawled around him on the grass of the Fernando Gordillo cultural center.

One of the youngsters asks him why he goes on writing when there is so much political work to be done in Latin America. Why doesn't he devote himself full-time to the Sandinista revolution, to the revolutions in El Salvador, Chile, Argentina? Julio defends himself, explains; they insist, and a discussion begins as to whether Cortázar should keep on writing or not. Nothing is closed to discussion in Nicaragua, and this has become a literary rally.

"To those who ask me to stop writing," Cortázar stands up—the tall Cortázar who never stopped growing —"I want to answer you with a Sandinista slogan: 'You shall not pass!'"

MAY 1982. PONELOYA

The morning when Tomás phoned to tell me of Julio's death, my wife and I talked and talked about him over breakfast, the shock giving way bit by bit to memories: the day she took Julio and Carol to Poneloya, a quick weekday excursion to the house above the rocks that is the scene of *Time of Splendor,* my first, long-ago novel. They eat lunch at the Salinas Relatives' Restaurant, an old, two-story wooden building with the first floor open on all four sides: stacks of firewood for the kitchen range piled around the tables; dogs, chickens, and in the center the stairwell leading to the second-story rooms where poor vacationers stay. Poneloya used to be an exclusive beach resort of private houses, most of which are now abandoned, deserted and crumbling, since their owners, free-spending cotton planters who gave all-night parties, have for the most part left for Miami.

While one of the relatives serves them (the elderly owner of the business and all his children are indiscriminately called "relatives" by the clientele), he asks Julio if he isn't by any chance the famous and renowned writer Julio Cortázar; and Julio is astonished, gratified, and smiling; and in a moment, from the cupboard where they keep the silverware and the plates, they brought back a dilapidated copy of *Hopscotch* (which isn't at all odd in a country where people recite Rubén Darío from memory in barbershops, at wakes, birthday parties, and in neighborhood bars: now, along with the divine swan, they pay homage to the divine tiger). In Poneloya again this summer, the relative told me, remembering Julio: I have never met a famous person as natural as the great novelist, the late Julio Cortázar.

The lunch ended. After eating, Julio went to sleep on a rusty cot without a mattress in the house above the rocks, and got up late to watch from the balcony the Pacific Ocean lit up by the violent flames of the sunset. Here, all sunsets are Darían, and the sea is always a vast mirror of quicksilver. The cross-hatching of the cotsprings stands out vividly on his back, proof of his tortured siesta by Nicaragua's bright Pacific.

JULY 19, 1982. MASAYA

Here we are, celebrating the third anniversary of the revolution. Since the beginning of the year, the CIA has been pulling out all the stops on its organ of terror, and we are now in open war. Blowing up bridges with plastic explosives, bombs in the baggage compartment of an Aeronica plane that leave several dead in the Sandino airport; Brenda Rocha, age 14, loses an arm defending a dam in Bonanza, fighting with a company of militia; this is the National War against the Filibusters, and anyone might tell you we're back in 1856. A Managua bricklayer—or was Andrés Castro a tailor?—killed a Yankee invader with a rock in the battle of San Jacinto because he'd run out of ammunition. But times change and we, besides having enough rocks, have a fair amount of ammunition. And good rifles.

Therefore, at this point in the championship match, it's the same to say, "All arms to the people," as to say, "All rocks to the people." Or as in Siuna or Bonanza, where the mines are now producing (you see, Mister Yankee, we could manage them all by ourselves), and where

Brenda Rocha, age 14, fought off the Filibusters, we might also say, "All brooms to the people."

Rifles, rocks, brooms. When they start coming, they shall not pass.

CORTÁZAR AMONG US

3. Plucking the eagle.

Having seen the foregoing propositions, we can conclude that the Latin American intellectual who best and most seriously saw and understood the Sandinista revolution as a Latin American phenomenon was Julio Cortázar; and, as a Latin American himself, he knew how to accept the consequences of his commitment. Yes, his commitment. Not the consequences in his literary work, for there might not have been any (though there were), but the consequences in his life, in his attitudes, and in his responses as an intellectual with a political position.

He knew that that proposition, of great propagandistic refinement, concerning freedom in the abstract and its philosophical variations, set amid the conglomeration of the Reagan administration's aggressive arguments, served North American military strategy just as much as its preparations for an invasion from Honduras, so that it too became part of the joint maneuvers. In the final analysis, Reagan is only fighting to give back to the Nicaraguans the freedom that the Sandinistas have snatched away from them and to rescue them from the communist inferno. And it also serves as a humanistic boomerang when it circles back to Europe and the United States itself to touch the western conscience in parliaments, academies, and newspapers: in Nicaragua they're chewing up the individual!

When a Latin American intellectual, a cultured and knowledgeable person from these parts, goes off to beguile western ears with this philosophical decoy, he is committing a brazen act of blackmail and is consciously playing to the eagle's rearguard, whose military strategy also requires the appropriate seduction of western consciousness: this eagle who doesn't have a single stupid feather to his name.

That is when our heroes put on taloned gloves and enter the lists, abandoning abstractions, because the purpose of their dissertations is to be believed and have Reagan believed.

And at that point, they speak to you not only of facts but of tendencies. Not only of what is, but of what can be. It isn't just that freedoms have been suppressed and the individual has been crushed, but that the philosophical conception of freedom and the individual that the Sandinistas secretly hold until they can apply it is a clear indication of their malevolent tendencies. Freedom and the individual will disappear in a near but uncertain future, because it is written in the entrails of birds that Nicaragua will sooner or later become a totalitarian county. And this being so, it is because the Sandinista project forms part of the great Soviet conspiracy for world domination. The virtue of this blackmail is to close the doors of the western paradise in your face, and from then on thou shalt earn thy bread in the sweat of thy brow.

And all for what? If you want to prove that you don't have totalitarian tendencies and that such thoughts have never entered your mind, then you have to accept the decoy—or the beguiling suggestion—that it is necessary to make a few more concessions to the eagle, to offer him a few more bleeding chicks by way of appeasement, while he circles, screeches, and sinks his claws into you; and in order that he doesn't go on believing that you have such tendencies, don't get so close to the Soviet Union, don't accept anything from them because what they want to do in the end is to seduce you, and may God keep you from accepting their oil; why do you need oil when candles will do? The eagle doesn't like communist electricity.

The confiscated revolution, some say. The betrayed revolution, say others. Where are the former owners of this revolution? Where are the betrayed lovers? This isn't melodrama; we receive their love letters every day, written in the blood of our nursing children destroyed by mortar shells, written in the blood of our mangled children who were just learning to walk. If you know of another type of humanism that we haven't heard about, come and explain it to us here, with all your western baggage.

And since we have totalitarian tendencies, we have also produced scarcity, shortages, lines, and all of this is due only to our hostility to western ideas. The Sandinistas have to prove, in order to be believed, that they are capable of surviving a war of foreign aggression while also maintaining abundance and prosperity.

When my Berlin friends told me their childhood memories of wartime, they didn't forget the potato-peel soup that was their daily lunch, nor their outings to collect roots, which they ate boiled: and all over Europe the lines to buy things that were nonexistent. In Nicaragua there are lines to buy gasoline; there isn't enough medicine, and imported articles are scarce; there are no automobile parts, and if the eagle keeps tightening the screws of the boycott, the few elevators that exist in Managua will soon stop functioning, and so will the air conditioning units.

But perhaps shortages, lines, scarcity are justified in a European war and are abnormal phenomena in a country without museums, without boulevards or opera houses to bomb, without factories manned by robots, and with so very few schools, without academies or symphony orchestras, or freeways or art galleries, but only humble Rural Infant Care Centers, Rural Supply Centers, Popular Agricultural Depots, Popular Education Centers, Oral Rehydration Units, which the guardian angels of western culture destroy every day and whose initials do not exist in the language of western civilization and therefore don't fall within a category of western Christianity.

Western categories that only have to do with the immutable being, armored in his ontological freedom from the moment he opens his newspaper at the breakfast table until he lays his head down on the pillow of tradition. No place for the will, the plans, the dreams of armed youths and militia women, of workers who argue and peasants who learn, of mothers in mourning, and dusty roads, scrub-wood thickets, wasteland, wilderness trails, clearings, mud, country roads, graves. Graves everywhere.

To end up by saying, "Your democracy is not a democracy," you held elections, but too late—you could have done that earlier; and now that you've finally held them, it's true that you won them, but you have to hold them all over again because it's never too late to sit down at the western banquet table.

Freedom yes, but the concrete thing, to touch it, to caress it like a sensual object, like a body, to test it, to mold it, to defend it. The reality of freedom, to extract it from the clay bank, fire it, give it form. And a humble democracy, extracted from the same bloodstained clay, kneaded by so many hands, don't ask me ahead of time what it looks like; I'll tell you when the clay has been fired. And meanwhile, if you don't help with the kneading, get out of the way.

There is that hole that has to be filled. Julio Cortázar setting foot on the waiting shore with its tortured headland. The signature of Julio Cortázar. We need Julio Cortázar.

JULY 1982. EL VELERO

Another Pacific coast beach in Nicaragua, warm volcanic sand and waves that break with a distant booming. We can see the terminal of the oil pipeline at Puerto Sandino (which used to be Puerto Somoza, naturally) that the CIA has tried so many times to destroy with underwater demolition charges, sea attacks, commando teams, *piranha* launches armed with cannon; they've tried everything.

Julio and Carol have withdrawn here to write, and they occupy one of the bungalows constructed for officials of Somoza's National Guard which nowadays house workers. The communal restaurant where you pay for your meals with tickets is almost in front of Julio's bungalow, across the blazing, treeless street. I see him from a distance, reading on the front porch; we're going to see each other later on this evening. But suddenly there is no later on. I am informed that the mercenaries have entered the small frontier village of San Francisco del Norte and massacred women, children, and peasant militiamen who defended themselves to the death against the invaders only a few hundred yards from the Honduran border, beyond which they have their hideouts. And Julio also has to return hastily to Managua with Carol, who is suddenly taken ill; precipitately and forever, Carol goes to Paris.

Carol Dunlop, with the trees full of children. She dazzled us with the impressions she had written about her trips to Nicaragua, an account Julio translated from the English to accompany her book of children's photographs that we published in the *Editorial Nueva Nicaragua* after her death; her photographs lovingly displayed one evening at Claribel's house, removed from their delicate wrappings and placed on tables, chairs, against the walls: a blessing of children, a loveliness of children, photographed on roads, in markets, rivers, neighborhoods, streets, vacant lots, trees; flocks of children. How can you make a revolution without children? That camera knew about children, and Carol Dunlop, who always walked through neighborhoods in search of children, the rivers of the Atlantic Coast in search of children; fences, whirlwinds, ponds, muddy streams, little wooden bridges across ditches, clothes hanging out to dry, blazing sun, sewing done here, embroidery done here, injections given here; this woman who caught the spirit of the revolution, these children who are never in our way, and why on earth haven't the Sandinistas ever formulated a birth control policy if there is so much poverty?

To keep on vaccinating them, of course. And to keep on taking their pictures.

FEBRUARY 6, 1983. MANAGUA

The revolution awards Julio Cortázar the Rubén Darío Order of Cultural Independence.

He has returned to Nicaragua for the first time without Carol. He has been with us since January, when the winds of solidarity brought him, along with Baptist ministers, civil rights leaders, US scientists, artists, and writers, to take part in a vigil in Bismuna, an indigenous community of North Zelaya that has just been wiped out by the counterrevolution. Julio goes where the revolution tells him to, a seasoned militant who pays no attention to categories, reputation, the company of peers, a celebrity who can be asked to travel to a remote village that was burned down a few days earlier and who stays up all night keeping vigil in the blackened ruins amidst songs, prayers, and speeches. Very few, perhaps none but Julio, would go off like that without first asking for a list of the participants and how many journalists and cameramen there would be. He never demanded peers even for signing a simple protest; you'd see his signature there standing out among all the rest, and his hand never trembled; he was always the same Julio, in pure solidarity, that he had been that first time in San José.

And it was during that January 1983 that he returned for the last time to Solentiname, his port of entry in the summer of '76, or what we call summer here, the grass dry and yellow, and the distant mountains ablaze with the fires before the next planting, smoke, sun, and the crickets chorusing in the burning plains, an oven-like lethargy and the perfume of *sacuanjoches*. And he retraced his path through the islands, the lake, the river; a jaguar chained to the dock at Santa Fe where the barges loaded with cattle leave for Diamante in Granada; the jungle restrained by the river's edge, a jaguar that licks the boots of the passenger as he gets off the boat. Had there been a peasant from Melchora who had seen him disembark next to the jaguar in the jungle by the river, and later had learned of his death, he would have said Julio was saying goodbye.

On presenting him with the decoration on that February night, the anniversary of Rubén Darío's birth, I spoke of Cortázar and Darío as heroes, both of them renovators of Latin American culture. It was a sober ceremony, without rhetoric or artifice, as are our Darían celebrations now. Daniel pinned the medal on his chest with simplicity, and he received it with simplicity; afterwards he read his speech.

He spoke of his debt to Darío, of the creative freedom in the revolution, of the flock of birds capable of changing the formation of their flight in mid-air without ceasing to be the same birds. Daniel whispered to me there on the dais that it was a very accurate image: when you're dealing with the same birds, art takes care of itself, and how beautiful are the changing formations in flight.

We like that recipe.

JULY 12, 1983. BELLO HORIZONTE

We're in the days of the fourth anniversary of the revolution, which we are going to celebrate in León. His Holiness Pope John Paul II has already passed through.

After a long day's work, I have gone to visit Julio in the house at Bello Horizonte in the eastern end of Managua, where he is staying as Tomás's guest. This is his last trip to Nicaragua.

We eat alone as the Managua night enters with its warmth and distant sounds through the half-open blinds, and we speak very professionally of matters of international solidarity: collecting signatures, communiqués, an old project of resident artists who would come to Nicaragua for a stay of weeks or months, working here and then telling of their experiences. We discuss this in detail. We already have a list with the names of García Márquez, Graham Greene, Carlos Fuentes, Gunther Grass, Pontecorvo, Theodorakis. To live the war and be able to film it, paint it, write it: these are the projects that in one way or another bogged down with his death. Also his participation in solidarity conferences, his constant responses in the European press to attacks on the revolution; we'll never again have so rigorous and tenacious a defender. We've rescued some of this in his book, *Nicaragua, So Violently Sweet.*

I ask him as we part why he doesn't come with me the following morning to El Ostional on the Costa Rican border where we are going to hand over agrarian reform deeds in a peasant ceremony. That is state terrorism, he tells me and laughs: agrarian reform on the Costa Rican border.

And of course I'll change all my plans, and we'll go.

JULY 13, 1983.
EL OSTIONAL / BELÉN

Rivas. On the narrow isthmus between the Great Lake of Nicaragua and the Pacific Ocean the only war of position we fought during the insurrectional campaign of May/July 1979 that ended with the defeat of the dictatorship's army. The Guard held the Pan-American Highway that borders the lake, and had fallen back to La Virgen just outside of the city of Rivas. The forces of the Southern Front had their closest advance units in Cárdenas, along the same highway, and from there to the sea they dominated the repetitive, softly rolling hills that reach down to the Pacific coast, all day long under Somocista artillery fire. Offshore, the hastily armed merchant ships of Somoza's Mamenic Line bombarded the hills, and in the outskirts of El Ostional the Guard had set up the *katiushkas* bought from the Argentine army.

Here we now celebrate the agrarian reform act beneath the unforgiving sun, amidst peasant militiamen with their brick-colored jackets and brick-colored faces, women in their Sunday best, rows of children, sun-faded red and black banners, posters with purple ink running down the Kraft paper. We are handing over the land to the frontier cooperatives.

Julio is sitting patiently on the platform, protected by the brim of a big straw hat; a truck-bed adorned with palm fronds and flowers serves as the rostrum. The microphone isn't working, and well into my speech I realize that nobody can hear me, and I have to start again without a microphone. I ask the peasants to come closer; it's enough to demoralize a person, but it works out well, and they are finally able to hear me. Julio laughs as he climbs down from the platform: you people never lose your cool.

In the tumult of departure, while we are pushing toward the vehicles amid outstretched hands, embraces, and placards, a woman dressed in mourning pushes through the crowd toward us; she has come from Belén, knowing that we'd be here, and she wants us to stop in Belén on the way back. Today is the anniversary of the massacre of Belén, and none of the Sandinista leaders has ever been there. She is the mother of one of the martyrs of Belén.

On July 13, 1979, when Comandante Exequiel—who was fighting in the rearguard of Somoza's forces with his peasant militia—had liberated the majority of the villages north of Rivas, a Guard patrol entered Belén, and the Guards, disguising themselves as Sandinista guerrillas with red and black kerchiefs around their necks, went through the streets calling on the young people to join the insurrection. The boys and girls came out of their houses eagerly: they were taken to the little plaza in front of the parochial church, and there, in the solitude of the night, they massacred all of them and threw their bodies into a well. Seventeen kids murdered.

Of course we'll pass through Belén after the inauguration of the mini-dam of Tola: another peasant ceremony beneath the three p.m. sun, to irrigate 700 *manzanas* belonging to the cooperatives that have been formed on the former feudal estates of Cornelio Hueck, president of Somoza's congress.

Then Belén, almost at nightfall. The streets are quiet and all the people are gathered around the well at one side of the plaza in front of the white church. The well is adorned with flowers, and next to it is a plaque with the names of the murdered youngsters. The priest finishes celebrating mass as the shadows gather, and he hands me the microphone. This time they can hear me.

Belén, Tola, Buenos Aires, Potosí, San Jorge, the domain of Comandante Exequiel, the school teacher. Never in the insurrection was there another tactical genius like him: a shadow, a shuttlecock moving behind the enemy lines. Now, as the darkness deepens, we walk in mid-street procession to the communal house where the mothers have prepared refreshments; in the corridor of the adobe house a table with embroidered tablecloth, loaded with pitchers, glasses, vases of flowers; and the mothers all busily at work in the kitchen.

I tell Julio that while inaugurating rural schools there in the same department of Rivas, from Salinas to Tola, I have had to eat seven meals in a single day; in each village there is always a lunch waiting, no matter what the hour: a hall adorned with tree branches and *chagüite* leaves and the lunch ready: humble houses in a bend of the road where the wind ruffles a lace curtain in the doorway, and they're waiting for you to eat lunch: the floor washed and polished, all the furniture piled in the patio to leave space for the table of honor with its tablecloth and flowers, pitchers of water, plates rescued from old cupboards all over the rural neighborhood.

We eat here amidst the faces of the mothers in the semi-darkness that the weak ceiling bulbs are unable to overcome. Attentive, serene faces worn out by sorrow; mothers of martyrs, dressed in black, my most constant and precise image of the revolution: the mothers, humble, cordial, stern; embracing them so many times, we have embraced poverty, embraced dignity, and there are so many of them. How many times have you felt yourself reviving, drawing strength from that embrace; when you feel dispirited, remember those embraces that also want to protect you, remember those eyes, reddened but defiant, remember that smell of sweat and mignonette, and the times you have heard them scream on receiving the bullet-riddled body of a child, while walking behind the flag-covered coffin, screaming with that rage that so often sustains us: *you god-damn sons of bitches!*

There is no other lament.

DAGUERREOTYPE

Father Gaspar García Laviana, of the Order of the Sacred Heart of Jesus, who, among other things, taught me one day that he also was a writer.

Gaspar came to Nicaragua as a missionary, and he settled down for a number of years as the parochial priest of Tola; and in those territories where Comandante Exequiel was later to rise up in arms, he preached the gospel and he preached the insurrection to the peasants of Las Salinas, the fishermen of Astillero, with whom he also built schools that can still be seen along the country roads.

One November day in 1977, I received a message in San José that somebody with the pseudonym of "The Buddha" wanted to contact the FSLN leadership; the Buddha was arriving from Guatemala, and when he left Nicaragua he had lost all contact with his clandestine organization.

The Buddha is the priest of Tola, Humberto told me, and we have to find him immediately. Two weeks earlier, he had been left waiting for an arms shipment for the two hundred peasants he had recruited in the area south of Rivas, and at the time of the attacks on San Carlos,

Masaya, Chinandega, and Ocotal, they were to have taken Rivas with the priest at their head. It was the offensive of October 1977, and the only one of the plans that failed was that of Rivas, for lack of arms.

The Buddha, his large square and hairy hands on the table at the Soda Palace where we talked the first time, with his heavy beard shaved in the style of an Asturian peasant, his vivacious deep black eyes beneath bristly brows, his hair shot through with gray, he was determined to immediately join the guerrilla forces of the Southern Front that were then being organized, to mobilize all of Rivas where the peasants were still awaiting their arms.

In December of that year, Humberto asked me to write a message that Gaspar was to sign at Christmas, explaining why he as a priest had chosen the path of armed struggle and was going off with the guerrillas, in hiding with the Sandinista Front.

We met in the San José safe house where Humberto lived secretly, to review the text of the message: the two of us seated on the edge of an unmade cot in the shadowy room. I read him the message I had written and that he was to sign. When I finished, he remained with his head between his hands, as concentrated as he had been during the reading. After a long silence, with an awkward and timid movement, he searched through his jacket pocket and finally pulled out some sheets of paper. He unfolded them uncertainly; his heavy handwriting crowded the pages.

He hesitated, folded the pages again, and, while he stuffed them back into his pocket, he told me that it was nothing important; as he was also a writer, he had worked on the text of the message. I insisted, his text had to be better than mine; I could never substitute for him in a matter of this sort; but there was no way to persuade him to pull out the sheets again; mine was enough. He was also a writer, but that was of no importance.

And you remembered this lesson that played such an important part in your life when, in asylum in the Mexican embassy in Managua, you saw the images of Gaspar's corpse transmitted triumphantly by Somoza's television that December of 1978. A year earlier he had walked out of that shadowy room after embracing you warmly, smilingly, leaving you crushed beneath the great peasant weight of his humility; and you remembered again, looking at the color photos found in the desk drawer of Somoza's chief of security: Gaspar's body, clad in olive green, lying on the grass, half of his face an enormous hole blown away by the bullet; only half a jaw covered with that stubborn shaved but still dark beard, only one vivacious dark eye beneath the bristly brow, the graying hair smeared with blood. You remembered that Gaspar also was a writer, that among other things he taught you one day that he also was a writer.

FEBRUARY 17, 1985 (SUNDAY) MONTPARNASSE

Now for the backward countdown. A year since Julio Cortázar's death, two years since we decorated him in Managua, and he told me that night he had never received so great and treasured an honor as that medal; the vigil among the smoldering houses of Bismuna and the lake breeze against his face in Solentiname, the miners in Siuna, the mothers of Belén; in a forest of arms, children are playing and life has captured every street. You see, Traveler, this is your open door.

We walk back toward the vehicles waiting in the alley, passing by the miniature shrines; we say goodbye to Tomasello, and on the way to the hotel to pick up our luggage Roberto Armijo tells me once again the final episode: he had been fighting to get them to take a photograph of Julio lying in his hospital bed, fighting for permission to make a death mask (so Central American, this thing of photos of the body and death masks; this character, Roque would have laughed, thinks he's dealing with the obsequies of Don Chico Gavidia).

But it was very important historically. Roberto managed at last to get the photographer in; it was midnight in the hospital corridors, everything was silent, and in the room the photographer set up his reflectors, tested the lights in the deathly solitude, adjusted his instruments, lenses, tripods. Julio is stretched out on the bed, serene, tranquil. Roberto, who had been there earlier, saw a faint smile on his lips. Beside him, on the night table, the last book he had been reading: a book by Rubén Darío.

The photographer set to work, shooting, seeking different angles in the room; one could hear only the click of the shutter, the soft humming of the motor as it rolled up the film. We've seen this photograph before. In *Blow-up*, wasn't it?

And what if you develop the roll and, instead of Julio lying there, you find Siuna, Solentiname, Bismuna, the mothers of Belén, a kid in an olive green uniform who tells you about a real war by the beach with the waves breaking before you?

A book by Rubén Darío, a flock of birds.

And now it's getting late, brother. The mothers of Belén are waiting for me.

Managua, March/June 1985

RELATED TITLES AVAILABLE FROM CURBSTONE

ASHES OF IZALCO, a novel by Claribel Alegría and Darwin J. Flakoll. A love story which unfolds during the bloody events of 1932, when 30,000 Indians and peasants were massacred in Izalco, El Salvador. $17.95cl. 0-915306-83-2; $9.95pa. 0-915306-84-0.

THE PATIENT IMPATIENCE, From Boyhood to Guerrilla: A Personal narrative of Nicaragua's Struggle for Liberation, by Tomás Borge. "A narrative about Nicaragua's revolution that is so trenchant, complete, and sensitive that it qualifies as history, biography and above all, poetry: an overwhelming amalgam of laughter and tears, triumphs and defeats, that leaves the reader delirious yet acutely aware of the reality of Nicaragua."—*Booklist.* $24.95cl. 0-915306-97-2

COSMIC CANTICLE, poems by Ernesto Cardenal. Written over a thirty year period, *Cosmic Canticle* is the crowning achievement of Ernesto Cardenal, one of the towering international figures in 20th century poetry. "Ernesto Cardenal is a major epic-historical poet, in the grand lineage of Central American prophet Ruben Darío." —Allen Ginsberg. $24.95cl. 1-880684-07-1

MIGUEL MARMOL, by Roque Dalton. Long considered a classic testimony throughout Latin America, *Miguel Marmol* gives a detailed account of Salvadoran history while telling the interesting and altogether human story of one man's life. $19.95cl. 0-915306-68-9; $12.95pa. 0-915306-67-0.

REBEL RADIO, The Story of El Salvador's Radio Venceremos, by José Ignacio López Vigil. This is an earthy, funny, inspiring oral history told by the participants in one of the most audacious and successful people's political actions in modern history. "....engrossing, self-effacing and hilarious."—*New York Times Book Review* $19.95cl. 1-880684-21-7

FOR A COMPLETE CATALOG, SEND A REQUEST TO:
Curbstone Press, 321 Jackson St., Willimantic, CT 06226

CURBSTONE PRESS

is a non-profit publishing house dedicated to literature that reflects a commitment to social change, with an emphasis on contemporary writing from Latin America and Latino communities in the United States. Curbstone presents writers who give voice to the unheard in a language that goes beyond denunciation to celebrate, honor and teach. Curbstone builds bridges between its writers and the public–from inner-city to rural areas, colleges to community centers, children to adults. Curbstone seeks out the highest aesthetic expression of the dedication to human rights and intercultural understanding: poetry, testimonials, novels, stories, photography.

This mission requires more than just producing books. It requires ensuring that as many people as possible know about these books and read them. To achieve this, a large portion of Curbstone's schedule is dedicated to arranging tours and programs for its authors, working with public school and university teachers to enrich curricula, reaching out to underserved audiences by donating books and conducting readings and community programs, and promoting discussion in the media. It is only through these combined efforts that literature can truly make a difference.

Curbstone Press, like all non-profit presses, depends on the support of individuals, foundations, and government agencies to bring you, the reader, works of literary merit and social significance which might not find a place in profit-driven publishing channels. Our sincere thanks to the many individuals who support this endeavor and to the following foundations and government agencies: ADCO Foundation, J. Walton Bissell Foundation, Inc., Witter Bynner Foundation for Poetry, Inc., Connecticut Commission on the Arts, Connecticut Arts Endowment Fund, Lannan Foundation, LEF Foundation, Lila Wallace-Reader's Digest Fund, The Andrew W. Mellon Foundation, National Endowment for the Arts, and The Plumsock Fund.

Please support Curbstone's efforts to present the diverse voices and views that make our culture richer. Tax-deductible donations can be made to Curbstone Press, 321 Jackson Street, Willimantic, Connecticut 06226. Telephone: (203) 423-5110.